BURMA

• Pagan

• Luang Prabang

L

V

Vientiane ▪

A

I

E

THAILAND

O

T

S

N

• Angkor

A

KAMPUCHEA

M

IMAGES OF ASIA
Series Adviser: SYLVIA FRASER-LU

Images of the Buddha in Thailand

Titles in the series

Images of the Buddha in Thailand

DOROTHY H. FICKLE

SINGAPORE
OXFORD UNIVERSITY PRESS
OXFORD NEW YORK

Oxford University Press

Oxford New York Toronto
Delhi Bombay Calcutta Madras Karachi
Petaling Jaya Singapore Hong Kong Tokyo
Nairobi Dar es Salaam Cape Town
Melbourne Auckland
and associated companies in
Berlin Ibadan

Oxford is a trade mark of Oxford University Press

ISBN 0 19 588920 7

Printed in Singapore by Kim Hup Lee Printing Co. Pte. Ltd.
Published by Oxford University Press Pte. Ltd.,
Unit 221, Ubi Avenue 4, Singapore 1440

To my husband, Lee

Preface

A visitor to a Buddhist country such as Thailand is soon overwhelmed by the number and variety of images of the Buddha encountered throughout the nation. In his initial bewilderment he wonders who is this being who has been represented. Why are images of him set up and worshipped in temples? Why does he reside on altars at home? Why is his image worn around the neck as an amulet? Why is there so much variation in the way he is depicted? What is the meaning of the serpent upon which he sits or the mythical animal upon which he rides? Why does he sometimes wear a crown and princely regalia? What is the bump on his head, the round dot on his forehead, the wheels on his hands or feet? These are the types of questions that this book has attempted to answer. In addition, the various styles of images that have evolved in Thailand have been examined and analysed, at the same time tracing their dependence on previous styles whether in Thailand or elsewhere.

The author wishes to thank the many individuals and institutions who assisted in the preparation of this book. Heartfelt gratitude is extended to Marc Wilson, Director, Nelson–Atkins Museum of Art, for permitting the writing of this book to intrude upon time for curatorial duties. Carol Stratton, Robert McNair Scott, and John Listopad have been most helpful in sharing their photograph collections. Other photographs were provided by the American Institute of Indian Studies in Varanasi, India, the British Museum, and the Nelson–Atkins Museum of Art. The Pali Text Society, Artibus Asiae, and Dharma Publishing have all permitted the use of copyrighted materials. Susanne Fickle happily drew the figures of hand gestures. Lee Fickle, Sonia Krug, and Janet Carpenter spent end-less hours editing the manuscript.

Kansas City   DOROTHY H. FICKLE
1988

Contents

I

Introduction

IMAGES of the Buddha are omnipresent in a Buddhist country such as Thailand. Upon entering a typical *bot* or *wihan*, the principal worship halls in a Thai monastery, one glimpses on a high dais opposite the main entrance an image of the Great Sage (Colour Plate 1), frequently gilded or decorated with flowers, scarves, or squares of gold leaf, surrounded by an array of other Buddhas, attendant figures, and gifts of all kinds. Incense, flowers, and candles have been placed on a table before the image, and people prostrate themselves as a sign of respect. On the interior walls of the temple often appear painted figures of the Buddha in scenes from his life history. Buddha images reside on a high shelf in homes, offices, and shops, and many Thai people wear amulets featuring a figure of the Buddha.

Who was the Buddha? Why is he so represented? The term 'Buddha', meaning 'the "Enlightened" or "Awakened" One', was originally an epithet for Siddhārtha Gautama (Pāli: Siddhattha Gotama), a historical person who lived in northern India from about 623 to 543 BC, according to Thai chronology, and who founded the religion known as Buddhism. Because Siddhārtha was born into the Shākya (Pāli: Sakyā) clan, he is also called 'Shākyamuni' (Pāli: Sakyamuni), the 'sage of the Shākyas'.

Indians have traditionally adopted a cyclical view of the natural world, including a belief in an endless cycle of rebirth. Each individual is reborn repeatedly into one of six possible states: that of a man, a god, a demigod, a wandering spirit, an animal, or in hell. His status and his location depend upon his own *karma* (Pāli: *kamma*)—his behaviour in previous lives. Most of these states of existence are thought of as miserable. Even a rebirth into heaven is not a source of happiness because a sojourn there is only temporary. Eventually the inhabitant of heaven will fall again into one of the lesser states. Any pleasure which he experiences will soon pass away, leaving him wretched again.

Shākyamuni learned through meditation that the cause of all this misery, sorrow, and pain is desire. The removal of desire results in the overcoming of pain. Desire can be eliminated through following a path combining ethical living, right knowledge, and meditation. An individual who understands the causal relationship between desire and pain and has succeeded in overcoming both can escape from the wheel of rebirth and achieve a state of eternal peace called *nirvāna* (Pāli: *nibbāna*).

Shākyamuni's own realization of this basic truth about reality is known as his enlightenment (*bodhi*). This understanding occurred when he was thirty-five years old. Henceforth he became known as the Buddha, 'the Enlightened One'. For the next forty-five years, he travelled throughout North India, preaching his doctrine to all who would listen. He died at the age of eighty or eighty-one, an event known as his *parinirvāna* ('final *nirvāna*'). Because he was able to escape from the cycle of rebirth, he no longer existed anywhere in the universe, and therefore could not be propitiated. He left behind his teaching, the Dharma (Pāli: Dhamma), and the order of monks he had founded, the Sangha. The latter was charged with carrying on the task of teaching the Buddha's message to all the world.

The earliest Buddhists recognized Shākyamuni as the latest in a line of Buddhas who had appeared successively on earth in order to preach the Truth. He was considered to be a human being and not a god, although he did possess a few supernormal powers, such as clairvoyance, knowledge of the past and future existences of all individuals, and the ability to perform miracles.

The monkhood gradually divided into sects, some of which

introduced new notions about the meaning of buddhahood. The Buddha became omniscient, and then transcendent. As a transcendent being, it was thought that he had never been of this world. His appearance on earth was seen as only an illusion, a device that enabled him to bring his message to mortals. He was never born, as he had always existed. He did not undergo enlightenment, as he had always been an enlightened being. He did not feel fatigue, become ill, or die. With these new concepts Buddhism evolved from an ethical and psychological teaching into a religion. These ideas eventually led to a new branch of Buddhism called the Mahāyāna (the 'Greater Vehicle'). The Mahāyānists later disparagingly labelled the earlier Buddhist sects as the 'Hīnayāna' (the 'Lesser Vehicle'). The Mahāyāna was destined to become the dominant Buddhist faith in northern Asia as well as in ancient Indonesia and Cambodia.

To the adherents of this new faith, the Buddha was thought to be ruling in divine radiance over a particular heaven, like a great emperor. The historical Buddha became one of an infinite number of Buddhas, each presiding over his own 'Buddha-field'. Each Buddha is a reflection of the ultimate reality which underlies the world that we experience. This ultimate reality is indescribable and can be known only through enlightenment. To achieve buddhahood, rather than to attain *nirvāna*, became the goal for each individual. Beings who have earned the right to future buddhahood are called bodhisattvas. As did the historical Buddha, they too practise the virtues that will lead to buddhahood. Meanwhile, in the manifested universe, the visible world that we all experience, the bodhisattvas aid all beings in attaining the same goal, thus exhibiting a more altruistic motivation than the Hīnayāna attempt to attain *nirvāna* for oneself alone.

An eternal, omnipotent Buddha watching over the universe was attractive to the masses, who longed for a deity to whom they could appeal for intercession and assistance. During the centuries just before and after Christ, a *bhakti* movement, involving an intense devotion to a personal deity, was gripping all of India, metamorphosing Hinduism as well as Buddhism. The earlier Buddhism had appealed primarily to those who were able to leave their homes to become monks, and discipline themselves to study and meditate. Now everyone could worship a transcendent Buddha with the hope that in a future life he might earn the right to become a Buddha himself.

So far we have encountered the individual Shākyamuni as one in a line of successive Buddhas, and also the concept of innumerable Buddhas each in his own 'Buddha-field'. Gradually, in the first few centuries AD, the Mahāyānists visualized a group of five specific great Buddhas, each known as a Jina ('victorious one'), or as a Tathāgata (a 'Thus-gone'), or 'one who has gone in the same way [as earlier Buddhas]'.[1] These Buddhas were recognized as cosmological and directional, with Vairocana in the centre, Akshobhya in the East, Ratnasambhava in the South, Amitābha in the West, and Amoghasiddhi in the North, each presiding over his own heaven. Associated with each were a large gathering of bodhisattvas and other deities, the most important being the compassionate bodhisattva, Avalokiteshvara, linked with the Buddha of the West, Amitābha.

The Mahāyānists also developed the idea of the three bodies of a Buddha. The Buddha in the ultimate, abstract sense is equivalent to his teaching, the Dharma. In this capacity he exists as the *dharmakāya* ('dharma-body'), which is formless and indescribable, and is shared by all the Buddhas. Because of its abstract nature, this form of the body of the Buddha cannot be depicted in art. When the Buddha preaches to the bodhisattvas, he is decorated like a prince, 'the body of enjoyment', the *sambhogakāya*. His image is then dressed in royal garb, wearing a

---

[1] Franklin Edgerton, *Buddhist Hybrid Sanskrit Dictionary*, Delhi, Motilal Banarsidass, 1972, p. 248.

crown, princely robes, and many ornaments. When the Buddha appears on earth to preach to the monks and to humanity in general, he assumes his 'body of appearance', the *nirmānakāya*, represented in art as a monk.

We have now discussed the Hīnayāna and the Mahāyāna. There was yet a third movement within Buddhism, the Vajra-yāna, 'the way of the *vajra*', also called Tantrayāna, 'the way of Tantra'. This branch of Buddhism became prominent in North-east India during the Pāla period, from the seventh to the eleventh centuries, and was destined to become the major form of Buddhism in Nepal and Tibet. It also survives in the Tendai and Shingon sects of Japanese Buddhism. The *vajra* (a 'thunder-bolt'), depicted in art as a short rod with prongs on both ends, was the symbol for the underlying reality which is equivalent to buddhahood. The Vajrayānists stress the role of ritual in attaining union with the divine. These rituals were eventually written down in texts called tantras.

In an attempt to emphasize the basic unity of the entire universe, the Vajrayāna created yet another great Buddha, the Adi-Buddha (the 'original Buddha'), a primordial being who represents the beginning of the creation of the manifested world, and who creates and presides over the group of five Tathāgatas developed earlier by the Mahāyānists. This third wave of Buddhism conceived an enormous pantheon of Buddhas, bodhisattvas, goddesses, demons, and mythical creatures of all kinds, who swarm through the thoughts and art of the peoples of the Himālaya.

The inhabitants of Thailand, both the populations who pre-ceded the Thai and the Thai themselves, have been adherents primarily of Hīnayāna sects. Since the thirteenth century, the dominant sect has been the Theravāda—the 'way of the elders'—a sect which was first introduced into Sri Lanka from India in the third century BC, and was brought to Thailand from Sri Lanka. The Theravāda is the root sect from which all others separated, and is believed to retain ideas closest to the original teachings of the Buddha. This is the only Hīnayāna sect that still survives today.

Because of these Hīnayānist beliefs, most of the images of the Buddha found in Thailand represent Shākyamuni, rather than a Tathāgata or the Adi-Buddha. However, at certain times during the history of the area, such as during the Indo-Javanese period on the Thai Peninsula from the eighth to the eleventh centuries, and the Khmer period in North-east and Central Thailand, especially in the eighth to the twelfth centuries, there was exposure to the Mahāyāna, resulting in images of bodhi-sattvas and the possibility that the Buddha images may represent one of the Tathāgatas rather than the historical Shākyamuni. Vajrayāna Buddhism existed at the Khmer monument, Prasat Phimai, in North-east Thailand, in the twelfth century, and there are traces of it on the Peninsula as well. However, images of the Adi-Buddha are exceedingly rare in Thailand.

To the Theravāda Buddhist, an image is intended to serve as a reminder of the Teacher and of his teachings. It theoreti-cally does not represent a supernatural being 'out there', waiting to be propitiated. However, the image on the altar in Thailand is obviously being worshipped by the devotee, who brings flowers and gifts, and bows low before it. The image has come to mean more to the people than a mere reminder of the teach-ing. It is treated as a deity, a Mahāyānist influence. Even in Theravādin literature, making and honouring Buddha images are lauded as important ways of gaining merit, adding to one's store of good that will enable one to achieve a higher rebirth and ultimately even the state of near annihilation called *nirvāna*. Sometimes images are buried inside monuments or other images, never to be seen, but their mere presence is believed to add to the merit of the persons responsible for the installation. Buddha images also serve as magic talismans, either for an individual in the form of an amulet, or for the state as the official palladium, expected to bring peace and prosperity to the kingdom. An example of the latter is the Emerald Buddha at Wat Phra Kaeo in Bangkok, which was installed by King Rama I when he made Bangkok the capital in the late eighteenth century.

The artist who produces an image of the Buddha does not have the goal of creating an original work of art. On the contrary he is working within clearly prescribed rules as to what the image should look like. He has studied a model, meditated upon it, and holding it firmly in his mind, deliberately attempted to copy it, in the belief that only in this way can he achieve a true likeness of the Buddha. Every image supposedly can be traced back through its many generations of antecedents to the historical Buddha himself. Over the centuries, it is true, an incredible variety of images of the Buddha have been produced, the result of a slow and steady stylistic evolution from the earliest images sculpted in India until the present day, and spread over the far-flung regions of Asia to which the Buddhist faith has penetrated, all reflecting local stylistic influences. In Thailand alone we shall encounter many styles.

All Buddha images possess certain common features. The Teacher is represented as a human being with one head and two arms, in contrast to the multi-headed, multi-armed images of many Hindu deities in India and the Vajrayānist deities of Nepal or Tibet. The Buddha is treated as a very special human being, even a transcendent one. The powerful body of the standing crowned Buddha from Ayutthaya (Colour Plate 19) and his gesture of offering protection suggest a lord who is very much in command of his world. He displays a special radiance that compels all beings to listen to his message. The half-closed eyes and serenity of the face and the body of the seated image from Prasat Phimai (Plate 5) promote a feeling of profound introspection and tranquillity. Tranquillity again, plus an infinite compassion and serenity, are imparted by the earlier Mon standing image from Central Thailand (Cover Plate). All of these suggest different aspects of the personality of this remarkable human being.

A seated Buddha is usually in a yogic posture, reflecting traditions that can be traced back in India to the Indus Civilization of the second millennium BC. Meditation—seeking the truth within oneself—is a vital ingredient of religious practice in India in all faiths. When the Buddha abandoned his princely life to become a religious wanderer, he discovered that listening to a teacher and practising extreme asceticism were not the methods that would lead to an understanding of the Truth. Rather, it was through meditation that he accomplished his goal. His actual enlightenment occurred after one final, extremely intense night of meditation. Meditation was an essential discipline for his followers if they, too, were to learn the Truth and attain *nirvāna*. The yogic posture—which suggests meditation—became a fundamental position for a Buddha image. The self-sufficiency and tranquillity of such a seated figure reflects the detachment from worldly concerns that typifies a Buddha once he has attained enlightenment.

The yogic posture can be depicted in two different ways. Throughout most of northern India and also in northern Thailand and in some cases on the Peninsula, the legs are fully crossed, with each foot lying on the opposite thigh in the 'adamantine pose' or *vajrāsana* (Colour Plate 13). At other times, especially in southern India, Sri Lanka, and South-East Asia, including most of Thailand, the right leg merely lies atop the left one in the 'hero pose' or *virāsana*, sometimes called *paryankāsana* (Plate 10). Very occasionally the Buddha sits in 'the European pose' with his legs hanging down (*pralambapadāsana*). Such a pose often signifies that he is at that moment actively engaged in the phenomenal world, preaching, teaching, or advising his followers, although such activities can be indicated with one of the yogic postures as well.

A Buddha image may also be represented standing, walking,

or lying down. Standing images are frequent, but the walking form is rare. A sculpture in the round of a walking Buddha was introduced during the Sukhothai period in the fourteenth century, and will be discussed in that context. A figure of the Buddha lying down represents his *parinirvāna* and is found in most schools of art.

The gestures performed by the hands of a Buddha image also have specific meanings which refer to some event in the life history of the Buddha. The six gestures that are most important throughout Asia are reproduced in the drawings of Figure 1. The *abhayamudrā*, with the hand held at chest or shoulder level, palm out, originally signified teaching, but later came to mean reassurance. The newer teaching gesture, *vitarkamudrā*, was similar except that the thumb and forefinger were joined. For preaching, and especially the preaching of the first sermon, the *dharmachakramudrā* is employed. The Buddha holds his two hands before his chest, the right hand palm outward, with the thumb and forefinger joined, touching one of the fingers of the left hand, held palm inward, also with thumb and forefinger joined. The gesture of giving charity, *varadamudrā*, features the hand extended downward, palm out. The gesture which represents the Buddha's enlightenment, *bhumisparshamudrā*—'touching the earth'—with the right hand palm inward touching the knee, illustrates an event that occurred as he meditated during the night of his enlightenment. With this gesture, Siddhārtha summoned the earth goddess Thoranee to witness the merit accrued throughout his many lifetimes and his right to achieve buddhahood. The final important gesture for a Buddha image is the *dhyānamudrā*—meditation—with the two hands, right over left, lying on the lap of a seated image.

Each of the great Tathāgatas or Jinas of the Mahāyāna pantheon displays one of these gestures. The Buddha of the centre, Vairocana, performs the *dharmachakramudrā*. Akshobhya, the Buddha of the East, sits in *bhumisparshamudrā*. The Buddha of

9

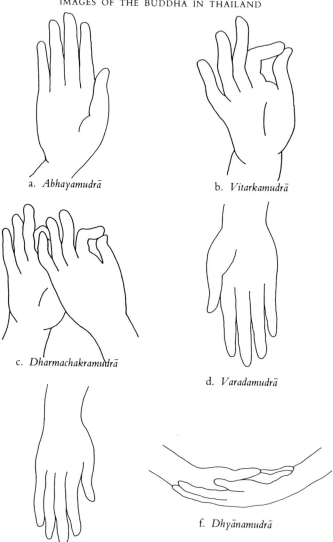

a. *Abhayamudrā*

b. *Vitarkamudrā*

c. *Dharmachakramudrā*

d. *Varadamudrā*

e. *Bhumisparshamudrā*

f. *Dhyānamudrā*

Figure 1. Hand Gestures of the Buddha. Drawings by Susanne Fickle.

the South, Ratnasambhava, holds his hand extended in the charity gesture (*varadamudrā*). Amitābha, the Buddha of the West, displays the *dhyānamudrā*. The Buddha of the North, Amoghasiddhi, is giving reassurance (*abhayamudrā*).

The people of Thailand have introduced certain peculiarities in the use of gestures on Buddha images. Frequently a standing image displays the teaching gesture with both hands, a custom which began at least twelve hundred years ago in the Chao Phya Valley, during a period when Mons were inhabiting that area. The original meaning of this double gesture is not known, but it came to signify the Buddha's descent from Tāvatimsa Heaven where he had gone to preach to his mother.

There are other unusual gestures which have had a more recent origin. During the nineteenth century, King Rama III (1824–51), wishing to perform an act of merit, attempted to systematize the iconography of the Buddha image. He requested the Prince Patriarch to select the principal episodes in the life of the Buddha and to suggest postures and gestures that could illustrate each one. A list of forty was drawn up, and the King commissioned the production of thirty-four of these images, omitting those that were already common. He had these new images installed in a small chapel in the compound of the Royal Chapel, planning that they should serve as iconographical models in the future production of Buddha images. However, these had little influence. They were not needed for the more common postures and the uncommon ones were ignored.

Three interesting new iconographies from this group involve the execution of the gesture of reassurance, *abhayamudrā*. This gesture performed by the right hand alone means that the Buddha is forbidding his relatives to dispute, a reference to an incident when the Buddha settled a quarrel over the division of irrigation water. The same gesture performed by the left hand alone means halting a sandalwood image. While the Buddha was absent in Tāvatimsa Heaven, King Pasenadi of

Kosala, according to legend, had an image of the Teacher created to serve as a reminder of him. When the Buddha returned, the image arose from its seat to advance toward the Buddha to pay homage, but he restrained it by raising his left hand. The image returned to its pedestal.[2] Performing the *abhayamudrā* with both hands signifies the calming of the waters, a reference to an incident when the Buddha was sojourning with the Kassapa brothers and was able to restrain the flooding Neranjarā River.

Most images of the Buddha display a few supernatural features. Sometimes there is a small round dot between the eyebrows, or a wheel may be seen on the palm of the upraised hand or on the soles of the feet. An unnatural bump may appear on the top of the head. The ears and the arms may be unnaturally long. These are examples of certain supernatural signs which were common in Indian iconography to all Great Persons (*mahāpurusha*), whether Universal Emperors (*chakravartin*) or Buddhas. There were thirty-two major signs (Sanskrit: *lakshana*; Pāli: *lakkhana*) and eighty minor ones (*anuvyānjana*). According to legend, just after the birth of the infant Siddhārtha, he was visited by the sage Asita, who saw the signs on the body of the child and realized his extraordinary nature.

These signs are enumerated in several Buddhist texts, both Pāli and Sanskrit. Here are the thirty-two major signs as listed in the *Dīgha Nikāya*, a sacred text of the Theravāda sect.[3]

And what, brethren, are the Thirty-two Marks of the Superman, wherewith endowed two careers lie open to him and none other: that of a Monarch, Turner of the Wheel...that of Buddha Supreme?

  (1) He hath feet with level tread. That this is so counts to him as one of the marks of the Superman.

  (2) Moreover beneath, on the soles of his feet, wheels appear

[2] Somphon Yupho, *Phra Phuttharup Pang Tang Tang (Various Iconographies of Buddha Images)*, Bangkok, Fine Arts Department, 1971, p. 71.

[3] T. W. and C. A. T. Rhys Davids, trans., *Dialogues of the Buddha*, Vol. III, London, Pali Text Society, 1977, pp. 137–9.

thousand-spoked, with tyre and hub, in every way complete and well divided. That this is so counts to him as one of the marks of the Superman.

(3) He has projecting heels. That this is so, etc.

(4) He is long in the fingers and toes. . . .

(5) Soft and tender in hands and feet. . . .

(6) With hands and feet like a net. . . .

(7) His ankles are like rounded shells. . . .

(8) His legs are like an antelope's. . . .

(9) Standing and without bending he can touch and rub his knees with either hand. . . .

(10) His male organs are concealed in a sheath. . . .

(11) His complexion is like bronze, the colour of gold. . . .

(12) His skin is so delicately smooth that no dust cleaves to his body. . . .

(13) The down on it grows in single hairs one to each pore. . . .

(14) The down on his body turns upward, every hair of it, blue black in colour like eye-paint, in little curling rings, curling to the right. . . .

(15) He has a frame divinely straight. . . .

(16) He has the seven convex surfaces. . . .

(17) The front half of his body is like a lion's. . . .

(18) There is no furrow between his shoulders. . . .

(19) His proportions have the symmetry of the banyan-tree: the length of his body is equal to the compass of his arms, and the compass of his arms is equal to his height. . . .

(20) His bust is equally rounded. . . .

(21) His taste is supremely acute. . . .

(22) His jaws are as a lion's. . . .

(23) He has forty teeth. . . .

(24) Regular teeth. . . .

(25) Continuous teeth. . . .

(26) The eyeteeth are very lustrous. . . .

(27) His tongue is long. . . .

(28) He has a divine voice like the karavīka bird's. . . .

(29) His eyes are intensely blue. . . .

(30) He has eyelashes like a cow's. . . .

(31) Between the eyebrows appears a hairy mole white and like soft cotton down. . . .

(32) His head is like a royal turban. . . .

The wheel (*chakra*), No. 2 on the list, symbolizes both the teaching of the Buddha, who turned the Wheel of the Law, and also the power of a universal emperor (*chakravartin*, 'the turner of the wheel'). The hairy mole, called an *ūrnā* (No. 31), usually sculpted as a round dot, is a mark of excellence. The royal turban (*ushnīsha*, No. 32) originally denoted the headgear of a prince, but gradually came to signify a protuberance on the head of the Buddha, a symbol of his great spiritual power and luminosity as well as his wisdom and knowledge. In East Asian symbolism, rays of light can emanate from both the *ūrnā* and the *ushnīsha*.

As time went on, more and more of the supernatural signs were incorporated into the images. The idea that the Buddha's hands are like a net (No. 6) resulted in a web between his fingers. The long fingers (No. 4) began to be interpreted as fingers of equal length (Colour Plate 1). The golden colour of the skin (No. 11) is depicted in many paintings, as well as through the gilding of images. Several of these supernatural signs became common in the art of Sukhothai in Thailand, such as the projecting heels (No. 3) and the arms extending to the knees (No. 9).

A general characteristic of a Buddha image is the arrangement of the hair in tiny snail-like curls that twist in a clockwise direction. This is undoubtedly based on sign No. 14; it is also one of the minor marks to be presented below. These curls first appeared on Buddha images in Mathura in India in the middle of the second century AD and rapidly became the most usual method of depicting the hair of the Buddha. According to legend, when the Buddha-to-be left his home, he cut off his hair with his own sword, and thenceforth it curled up in this fashion and never required cutting again. Turning in a clockwise or sunwise direction is an auspicious sign in Indian thought.

Worshippers encircle a revered monument in a sunwise direction, for example, keeping the hallowed object on their right.

The eighty secondary marks that appear on the body of a Great Person are presented here as translated by Gwendolyn Bays from the *Lalitavistara*, a Sanskrit biography of the Buddha dating back to approximately the first century AD.[4] The name for the young Buddha-to-be in this passage is Sarvārthasiddha, 'one who has accomplished all aims'.

The young Sarvārthasiddha has rounded fingernails, O Great King, glossy and the color of red copper. His fingers and toes are long and very fine and tapering. His veins and ankle bones are hidden. His joints are solid; his feet smooth and regular; his heels broad.

O Your Majesty, the lines in young Sarvārthasiddha's hands are smooth, equal, regular, deep, and long. His lips are red like the fruit of the bimba, his voice well-modulated, not too high. His tongue is soft and delicate, the color of red copper. His sweet and beautiful voice sounds like the cry of an elephant, like thunder. O Great King, the young Sarvārthasiddha's sexual organs are complete. His arms are long, his limbs are broad and well-covered, his skin is soft. His body is not subject to fear or disquiet; it is well-proportioned, beautiful, and heroic. His limbs are perfect; his knees broad, strong, and well-developed.

O Great King, the young Sarvārthasiddha's body is rounded and elegant, straight, smooth, and beautiful. His navel is deep, straight, and regular. Like a rishi [sage], he is pure in conduct; his appearance is beautiful and pure, radiating such light that it dispels the shadows. Great King, young Siddhārtha moves with the dignity of a bull. He has the majestic gait of the elephant, O Great King, and the heroic walk of the lion. He has the powerful gait of the great bull, and moves like the flight of the goose. He walks always turning toward the right.

The sides of his body are rounded, elegant, and symmetrical, and his waist is like the curve of a bow. O Great King, the brilliance of the young Sarvārthasiddha's body is untarnished—not a dark spot mars

---

[4] *The Voice of the Buddha: The Beauty of Compassion*, Vol. I, Berkeley, Dharma Publishing, 1983, pp. 156–7.

its beauty. His front teeth are rounded, his eyeteeth are pointed, his molars are regular. His nose is sharply defined; his brilliant, clear eyes are smiling, elongated, and large, like the petals of the blue lotus.

The young Sarvārthasiddha, Great King, has eyebrows which are even, beautiful, dark, connected, and smoothly arched. His cheeks are full and even, free from imperfection. With his senses perfectly controlled, he is free from hostility and wrath. The sense organs of the young Sarvārthasiddha, O Great King, are perfect and complete. He has a face and a forehead in harmony with each other, and his head is well-developed. His hair is full-bodied, falling freely from his face and brow, well-arranged, smooth, and black. Sweet in smell and luxuriant, it is never unkempt or tangled, but is very fine and curly. The hair of the young Sarvārthasiddha, O Great King, curls [in a clockwise direction].

According to these literary descriptions of the body of the Buddha, an image should be perfectly proportioned, symmetrical, smooth, and fully rounded, with broad shoulders and narrow hips. There should be no sign of muscles, veins, or bones. His torso should be like that of a lion, his legs like a gazelle, his arms like the trunk of an elephant. Of course, many of the elements of these descriptions cannot be incorporated into an image, such as the number of teeth, the sound of his voice, or the way he walks.

There are several characteristics of Buddha images which are not specified in any text, and yet are almost universally portrayed. One of these is the length of the ears. The exaggerated size of the ear suggests the Buddha's supernatural ability to hear everything in the universe. Or the long ear lobes may be due to the heavy ear-rings that the young prince Siddhārtha would have worn before he became a spiritual recluse.

Another traditional mark that is not mentioned in the texts is the series of three lines on the neck. These have been interpreted both as beauty marks and as signs of greatness. The moustache, common in some Thai styles, such as the art of Lop Buri, Haripunjaya, and Ayutthaya, is another anomaly.

An outstanding characteristic of the Buddha was his radiance. This could be suggested in a variety of ways. In Indian art an image of the Buddha often includes both a halo behind his head and a mandorla surrounding his body. These are rare in Thailand. In both Indian and Thai art, a flame or a jewel may rise from the *ushnīsha*. In East Asian paintings, rays of light are seen issuing from the *ūrnā* or *ushnīsha*. The luminosity of his skin is said to have rendered his clothing transparent. On images, therefore, the robe is sometimes visible only at the neckline, wrists, and ankles. The golden hue of a painted image or the gilt of a bronze can also suggest his supernatural radiance.

Let us now examine some of the Buddha images that have been found in Thailand, to determine how these general ideas about the nature of the Buddha have been interpreted in Thai art.

Pre-Thai Images of the Buddha

Art Styles in Thailand

THE images of the Buddha discussed in this book have been
classified on the basis of a scheme first proposed by Piriya Krairiksh in 1977[1] and refined in 1979.[2] Piriya's scheme is presented
in the first column of the following table. The second column
lists the more traditional periods of Thai art proposed in 1926
by HRH Prince Damrong Rajanubhab, as employed by
M. C. Subhadradis Diskul.[3]

The Classification of Thai Sculpture

Piriya's Scheme	*Standard Scheme*
	Imported objects discovered in Thailand, *c.*AD 1st–11th c.
	Ancient Hindu images, 7th–9th c.
Peninsular styles:	Srivijaya style, 8th–13th c.
South, 3rd–13th c.	
Mon styles:	Dvaravati style, 6th or 7th–11th c.
Centre, 6th–10th c.	
North-east, 8th–10th c.	
North, 10th–13th c.	
Khmer styles:	Lop Buri style, 7th–14th c.
North-east, 6th–14th c.	
Centre, 10th–13th c.	
Thai styles:	
Lan Na (north), 13th–19th c.	Chiang Saen or northern Thai style, *c.*11th–18th c.

[1] *Art Styles in Thailand*, Bangkok, Fine Arts Department.

[2] *The Sacred Image: Sculpture from Thailand*, Cologne, Museum for East-Asian Art.

[3] *Art in Thailand: A Brief History*, 6th ed., Bangkok, Amarin Press, 1986.

Sukhothai (north-centre), 13th–15th c.	Sukhothai style, late 13th–early 15th c.
Lop Buri (centre), 13th–14th c.	
Suphan Buri/Sankhaburi (west-centre), 13th–14th c.	U Thong style, c.12th–15th c.
Ayutthaya (centre), 14th–18th c.	Ayutthaya style, mid-14th–mid-18th c.
Ratanakosin (centre), 18th c.– the present	Ratanakosin style, late 18th– early 20th c.

To Prince Damrong the categories for the classification of Thai sculpture were tentative, but they were repeated by subsequent scholars and continued in use until the present. There are many flaws in this standard system. Two of the art styles were named for ancient kingdoms, Dvaravati and Srivijaya, both of which are only vaguely known and whose territory clearly did not encompass the entire area from which art works so-labelled emanated. The art which related to that of the ancient Khmer empire was named after Lop Buri, a provincial capital during the Khmer occupation of Central Thailand. Yet Khmer-related works of art have been found elsewhere in Thailand in addition to Lop Buri. Furthermore, the art discovered at Lop Buri reflects several different styles over a period of time. Chiang Saen, the name of one small principality, was applied to the art of all of North Thailand, another misnomer. Furthermore, in Prince Damrong's scheme, Hindu art was separated into a category of its own, even though stylistically Hindu art and Buddhist art can be identical.

Piriya Krairiksh's system of classification divides the art initially on ethnical considerations and then subdivides it on the basis of geography. There are three ethnical groups which produced styles of art distinctive from each other—the Mon, the Khmer, and the Thai. The Mon seem to have been the principal inhabitants of the area that is now Central Thailand during the first millennium AD. Art in the Mon style has also been located

in North-east Thailand, and there was a late Mon culture surviving at Haripunjaya in North Thailand until the thirteenth
century. Khmer art was produced during periods when the
Khmer extended their control over parts of Thailand. Some
of it emanated from the political centre at Angkor and other
objects were locally produced in Thailand under Khmer influence. The Thai people, who were latecomers in achieving
political power in Thailand, began their artistic productions
in the thirteenth century, continuing to the present. Piriya
places the art of Peninsular Thailand into a fourth category by
itself.

The major criticism aimed at Piriya's classification scheme
is that there is no certainty that the three ethnical groups—the
Mon, Khmer, and Thai—really did produce the art so classified.
However, his scheme seems to fit the material remains better
than the earlier classification scheme. Piriya further subdivided
the two categories of Peninsular art and Khmer art in subsequent publications.[4] We shall encounter these ideas as we survey
the relevant categories below.

Let us begin our discussion of the Buddha images of Thailand by looking at two imported images, one from Sri Lanka
and the other from India, and then move on to the Mon, Khmer,
and Peninsular styles. In the following chapter we shall examine the images produced by the Thai.

Imported Images

A few images have been discovered throughout South-East
Asia, including Thailand, that appear to have been early imports
from India or Sri Lanka. The first example we shall examine is
a small bronze found at Korat, Nakhon Ratchasima Province,

---

[4] *Art in Peninsular Thailand Prior to the Fourteenth Century A.D.*, Bangkok, Fine Arts
Department, 1980 and *Khmer Bronzes*, Lugano, Italy, Corner Bank, *c.*1984.

North-east Thailand (Colour Plate 2), now in the Bangkok National Museum. The right arm and hand, the feet, and the pedestal are all modern restorations. This image bears a close relationship to the Buddha images of both Sri Lanka and the Andhra region of the South Indian Deccan of about the seventh to eight centuries. Its robe is draped in a fashion typical of the images of both these areas, but rare in Thailand, where most Buddha images follow the drapery styles of North Indian prototypes. This southern method of draping the robe has been categorized by A. B. Griswold as the 'Mathuran mode', named after the practice demonstrated by certain images of the second and third centuries AD produced in the Mathuran region of North India.

According to the Buddhist texts, a monk, and consequently a Buddha, should wear three garments (Sanskrit: *tricīvara*; Pāli: *ticīvara*). He begins with an undercloth (*antaravāsaka*), a large rectangular piece of cloth that is draped around the lower half of the body, with the excess material arranged into pleats either in the centre front or at one or both sides. At the waistline the undercloth is folded over a belt (see Figure 2a-d). On the Korat Buddha, this undercloth can be detected at the bottom falling below the front part of the outer robe, with its pleats visible just to the left of the Buddha's left leg.

The second garment, the robe (*uttarāsanga*), is also a rectangular piece of cloth. In the Mathuran mode, the end of the material is first bunched up and held in the left hand (Figure 3a). The long side is placed over the left shoulder, across the back, and under the right arm. It is thereupon gathered together and the entire robe flung back over the left shoulder and allowed to fall freely to the bottom in the back (see Figure 3b, c). The original gathered edge of the robe can be seen in the left hand of the Korat Buddha, and the lower corner of the flung-back portion is visible at the Buddha's lower left. A back view of this image from Korat resembles the sketch of Figure 3c.

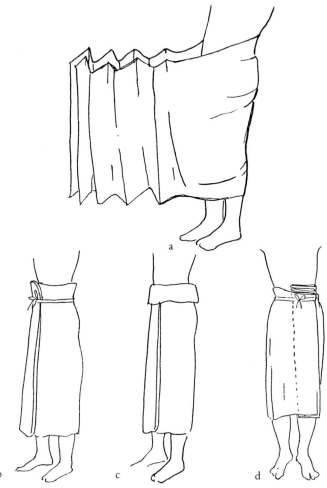

Figure 2. The Undercloth of a Monk.
   a. Composition of the panel.
   b. Frontal panel, with belt.
   c. Frontal panel, with overhang covering belt.
   d. Lateral panel, turned inward.
Drawings after A. B. Griswold, 'Prolegomena to the Study of the Buddha's Dress...', *Artibus Asiae*, Vol. XXVI, No. 1, 1963, Fig. 1.

Figure 3. The Robe of a Monk, 'Mathuran' Scheme.
    a. Preparatory position.
    b. Final position.
    c. Rear view of final position.
Drawings after A. B. Griswold, 'Imported Images and the Nature of Copying in the Art of Siam', *Essays Offered to G. H. Luce*, Vol. II, Artibus Asiae Supplementum 23, 1966, Fig. 4.

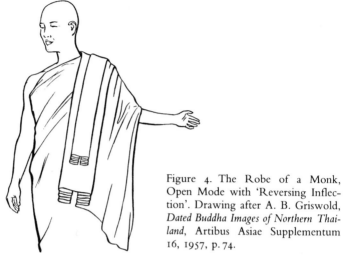

Figure 4. The Robe of a Monk, Open Mode with 'Reversing Inflection'. Drawing after A. B. Griswold, *Dated Buddha Images of Northern Thailand*, Artibus Asiae Supplementum 16, 1957, p. 74.

The third garment traditionally worn by a monk is the shawl (*sanghāṭī*), a piece of material identical to the robe. If both the robe and shawl were being worn, the robe would be entirely hidden by the shawl. Sometimes a double line at the neck suggests the presence of both garments. In a warm country such as Thailand, the shawl is usually carried as a spare garment, folded and placed over the left shoulder (Figure 4 and Colour Plate 17). This image from Korat does not wear the third garment.

Early writers generally associated the bronze from Korat with second- to third-century images found in the Amaravati area of South India. The large size of the curls and the rounded folds of the robe do relate to Amaravati. However, recent scholarship inclines toward a Sri Lankan origin on the basis of the expression of the face, the flat locks of hair, the small mouth, and the lack of an *ūrṇā*. The image is also now generally assigned to a later date. In both Amaravati and Sri Lanka, the early images did not reveal the contours of the body. Such modelling represents an influence from the fifth-century Gupta art of North India (see Colour Plate 4). Because of the presence of this modelling on the Korat Buddha and also because it has a flame finial surmounting the *ushnīsha*, which did not appear in Sri Lanka or anywhere else before the eighth century, this image should be dated to the eighth century at the earliest.

The style of image represented by the Korat bronze had very little influence in Thailand. A similar imported one has been found at Sungai Kolok in the extreme south of the Peninsula, and a local copy was produced at Nakhon Pathom. A few other fragments have been found. However, most of the imagery of Thailand had a North Indian prototype.

A sandstone Buddha image, found in Wiang Sa District, Surat Thani Province, on the Thai Peninsula (Colour Plate 3), now in the Bangkok National Museum, is close in style to the Gupta art produced at Sarnath in North India in the fifth century AD (compare with Colour Plate 4). Sarnath is the name of a park near the present Varanasi in the Ganges Valley where the Buddha preached his first sermon. It became an important pilgrimage site after the *parinirvāna* of the Buddha, along with the sites of his birth at Kapilavastu, now in Nepal, his enlightenment at Bodhgaya, and his death at Kusinara. During the Gupta period, in the late fourth to the fifth century, Sarnath was the location of an important monastery, which became the centre of a school of Buddhist sculpture employing a cream-coloured sandstone to create images of supreme sensitivity and beauty. The Sarnath style had its roots in the Kushana art of the Mathura region, a little to the west in North India. The Gupta-period art of the Sarnath area influenced the subsequent development of Buddhist sculpture throughout Asia, including Thailand. We shall witness this influence principally in the Wiang Sa image we are now examining and in the Mon style of Central Thailand, to be discussed in the next section.

Both the Wiang Sa and Sarnath images stand in high relief against an arch-shaped backpiece, demonstrating a slight triple flexion of the body (*tribhanga*), and holding their right hands downward in the gesture of charity (*varadamudrā*). The left hand is missing in each case, but probably was lifted up and holding a corner of the robe, the usual manner for Gupta images. Both the method of draping the robe and the modelling of the body distinguish this image from the South Indian–Sri Lankan style typified by the Korat bronze Buddha.

The robes of both the Wiang Sa and Sarnath images have been draped in a manner which Griswold labelled the 'Gandharan mode' (Figure 5), displayed by the second- to third-century Buddha images from Gandhara, the ancient name for an area that now straddles northern Pakistan and Afghanistan. This is the fashion followed most widely throughout Northeast India and also in the images of Thailand. In this method, the left hand holds only the upper corner of the robe instead of

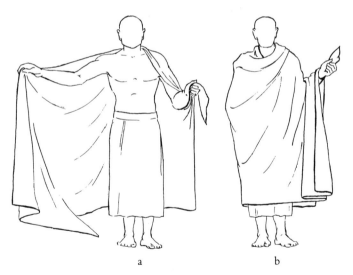

a   b

Figure 5. The Robe of a Monk, 'Gandharan' Scheme in the Covering Mode.
a. Preparatory position.
b. Final, with right hand muffled.

the entire bunched-up end, the rest of the end falling straight down to the lower hem (Figure 5a). The robe is then led back across the left shoulder, forward over the right, then straight across the front of the body and over the left arm, the upper corner falling over the left shoulder in the back, stopping at mid-level (Figure 5d), while the lower corner is lined up in front evenly with the initial lower hem (Figure 5c). Any excess material forms a pleat or lappet on the left side. To free the right arm, which is at first engulfed by the robe, the material is lifted up over the right forearm (Figure 5c). The lower hem of the robe on the right side thereby forms a circumflex inflection, like an inverted V. Sometimes, to secure the robe more firmly, the end that has been thrown over the left shoulder is brought back toward the front under the elbow and held in the left hand, along with the original corner this hand is already holding.

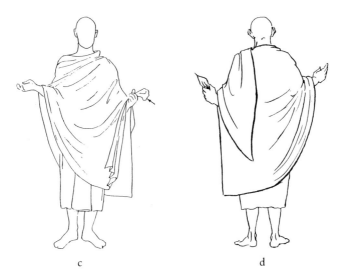

c

d

c. Circumflex inflection.
d. Circumflex inflection, rear view.
Drawings after Griswold, 'Prolegomena', Fig. 2.

The method of draping just described results in the covering of both shoulders. The right shoulder can be exposed by draping the robe in exactly the same fashion, except that the upper edge of the robe is brought under the right arm instead of over it (Figure 6).

The Wiang Sa and Sarnath images have both been draped in this Gandharan mode, with the robe covering both shoulders. The broken left hand of each image probably held the initial upper corner of the robe and possibly the final upper corner as well, brought back around under the elbow to the hand. The two lower corners can be seen in a damaged state at the Buddha's lower left on the Sarnath image. The right hands of both images have been thrust out from beneath the robe, drawing it up to create a circumflex curve. The two lower corners on the Sarnath

Figure 6. The Robe of a Monk, 'Gandharan' Scheme in the Open Mode. Drawing after Griswold, 'Prolegomena', Fig. 3.

Buddha's right, therefore, which represent an intermediary portion of the robe, are curved in contrast to the two pointed corners visible on his left, which portray the true ends of the piece of fabric. According to the Buddhist canon, the lower hem of both the front and the back of the robe should be at the same level, but in a process called anamorphosis, the artist has lowered the back hem of the Sarnath image so that we can see it. The undergarment is lower still. The lower edge of the Wiang Sa image has been broken off, but that which remains indicates these edges were executed in the same manner as the image from Sarnath.

A distinctive feature of the Sarnath Gupta style of Buddha image is the clinging of the sheer robe to reveal the contours of the body. This characteristic is often labelled the 'wet look'. No folds of the robe are visible. The robe can be detected only at the neckline, wrists, sides, and along the hemline. The top of the undergarment is indicated by an incised line at the waist and a slight swelling of the abdomen above this line. These characteristics are all repeated on the image from Wiang Sa.

The hair of the Sarnath Buddha is arranged in the small curls typical of the Gupta period. The curls are lined up in even rows across the head, with a slight dip at the centre. The cylindrical *ushnīsha* is more pronounced than on the images of South India and Sri Lanka. The figure has the usual long ears and the three lines on the neck. There is no *ūrnā*. The lips curve in a gentle smile. The eyes are downcast. The expression on the face is highly spiritual, serene, and self-contained. The broad shoulders, narrow waist, and webbed fingers are other features of a Great Person.

The Buddha from Wiang Sa follows the Gupta model closely, especially in the use of high relief and in the posture and gestures, the manner of draping the robe, and the visibility of the body contours through the robe. The *ushnīsha* is flatter, however, more akin to the South Indian and Sri Lankan styles.

The curls too are flatter and the features of the face more delicate. For these reasons, this sculpture may not have been an import but a direct copy of a Gupta model produced locally on the Thai Peninsula, where South Indian and Sri Lankan models were also available. It should be dated to the late fifth century AD.

Mon Styles

During the first millennium AD, the Mons were the people residing in the river basins of Central Thailand, as attested by inscriptions. They seem to have been organized into a number of small city-states, the best known being Dvaravati. Important Mon centres of Central Thailand include Nakhon Pathom, Lop Buri, U Thong, and Ku Bua. Mon-style art has been found in North-east Thailand as well, although whether Mon kingdoms existed there is not known. There was a late Mon kingdom at Haripunjaya in North Thailand, however, where many archaeological remains have survived.

The classical Mon-style Buddha image has derived from the Gupta Sarnath style (compare the Cover Plate and Colour Plate 4), perhaps with the further intermediation of the style produced in the caves of West India under the Vakatakas, contemporaries of the Guptas, whose art was closely influenced by Gupta art (Plate 1). These cave Buddhas, especially the standing ones, are more formal and abstract and generally less languid than the Sarnath images. The typical Mon Buddha (Cover Plate) is free-standing, having abandoned the backpiece, although the image has been designed to be viewed frontally. The back and the sides are only cursorily sculpted. The Mon Buddha, depicted as asexual, displays a body rendered with the wet nude look encountered in Gupta art. The robe has been draped in the Gandharan mode, covering both shoulders. There is no line around the neck to indicate the top of the robe (the

1. Façade detail to left of door, Ajanta, Cave 19. Vakataka period, late fifth century. Photograph courtesy of the American Institute of Indian Studies and the Archaeological Survey of India.

lines we see are beauty marks), but the draping about the arms and at the lower left lets us know the figure is clothed. There is a swelling across the abdomen to indicate the top of the undergarment. The anamorphosis is more exaggerated, as now the back of the robe falls below the undergarment, and considerably below the front of the robe. The final lower front corner has been lifted and held by the left hand, causing a curve at the lower left to match the usual one at the lower right, here broken off. The two curves together would have created a scarf-like U across the calves of the image. This manner of draping is a result of the Mon love of symmetry.

Symmetry is also achieved through having the two arms perform the same gesture, usually *vitarkamudrā*. Unfortunately, both arms are now broken off, often true of the surviving Mon stone standing images. However, the remaining portions of the arms suggest that they both were once held in the same fashion. We can visualize the complete iconography by examining a typical Mon bronze image, with its two hands in the double *vitarkamudrā* (Colour Plate 5). It is believed that the prevalence of the teaching gesture in the Mon art of Thailand was a Sri Lankan influence, as this gesture was comparatively rare in India.

The hair of the Mon stone sculpture is rendered in large, flat, spiral curls with a low conical *ushnīsha*, slightly lower than the more cylindrical Sarnath *ushnīsha*. This low *ushnīsha* may again be a South Indian or Sri Lankan influence. The Mon face is round with high cheek-bones. The eyebrows are sculpted as a low ridge which is connected over the bridge of the nose and arches upward over each eye, often compared to the wings of a swallow. The eyes are shaped like lotus petals, pointing downwards toward the nose and upwards toward the temples, with the lids lowered. The nose is flat. The mouth is shaped like a bow and gently smiling. The gentility, serenity, and compassion expressed by this Buddha's face combine to impart a feeling of great spirituality. This sculpture probably originated in Lop Buri, the site of the earliest Mon images, and can be dated to about the seventh century.

The bronze image (Colour Plate 5) also demonstrates the nude asexuality and the complete symmetry that are typical of the Mon Buddhas. The two hands both perform the teaching gesture. The edges of the robe, which covers both shoulders, are arranged evenly on both sides, resulting in a U-inflection at the front. The undergarment is not revealed at the waist nor at the lower edge, unless the ridge of cloth at the bottom is supposed to suggest this garment. The Buddha stands rigidly, with no movement to his body. His curls are smaller than those of the stone image. His cylindrical *ushnīsha* is more fully developed, comparable to that of the Sarnath Buddha. His facial features are less subtly executed compared to the stone Buddha from Dvaravati, and his eyebrows are not joined. This small bronze can be dated to about the eighth century.

Some Mon-style Buddha images were also produced on the Thai Peninsula. An example dating to perhaps the eighth century can be seen in Colour Plate 6. This image originated at Wat Yai, Ban Ko, in Nakhon Si Thammarat Province, and is now at Wat Mahathat in Nakhon Si Thammarat. The figure is more rigid and less natural than the two Mon images from Central Thailand. This may reflect a greater influence from the Indian Vakataka (Post-Gupta) sculptural style of the cave temples of western India, as represented by the two frontally standing images in the illustration from Ajanta in Plate 1. Both the Mon and the Ajanta images are similarly stocky and hieratical. The Mon example has transformed the Vakataka prototype into a completely symmetrical image. The two Ajanta Buddhas have their robes draped over one shoulder only, and the two hands perform different gestures. The robe of the Mon image has been draped covering both shoulders, and the edges have been made identical on both sides, resulting in a pronounced U-inflection of the lower edge of the robe. A line now marks the top of the undergarment. The *ushnīsha* is now higher and more cylindrical than on the stone Buddha from Central Thailand. It is more closely akin to the Gupta fashion. The face is more square. The curving joined eyebrows are retained. The eyes are still half closed. The nose is flat, and the lips are large. The face has acquired the characteristics of the Mon people. This image has retained one of its hands. It is assumed that the other hand executed the same gesture.

The typical Mon image in Thailand is the standing type we have been describing. Seated images were more rare, but a few examples are known, some with the two legs hanging down in the so-called European position (*pralambapādāsana*) and others with the two legs folded right over left (*virāsana*). An example of the latter is the Buddha sheltered by the *nāga* (seven-headed serpent) depicted in Colour Plate 7, a relief sculpture which originated in Dong Si Maha Pot, Prachinburi, now in the Bangkok National Museum. The iconographic theme of a Buddha being sheltered by the naga is occasionally encountered in the Mon art of Thailand, but more frequently in Khmer art. Such an image usually illustrates an event which occurred during the third week after the Buddha's enlightenment. He was sitting in deep meditation on the shore of a lake when a storm arose, causing the waters to rise, threatening to engulf him. The serpent king (*nāgarāja*) Muchalinda rose up from the depths of the lake, coiled himself around the Buddha, and spread his hood over him to protect him from the elements. In art the Buddha is usually shown seated on the coils of the naga rather than enclosed by them, and the hoods are spread over his head. The coils of the naga have not been depicted on this Mon relief slab from Dong Si Maha Pot. Only the naga hood, with its seven heads, is present.

A few sculptured examples of the Buddha being protected by the naga are found in the Amaravati art of the Andhra area,

South India, but always as an incidental part of a relief. Individual images featuring this iconography began in Sri Lanka. Both the Mon images and those from Sri Lanka are similar in the use of the *virāsana* posture and the meditation gesture (*dhyānamudrā*), the draping of the robe covering the left shoulder only, and the arrangement of the seven heads of the naga's hood. The variation of the posture in which the legs of the Mon image are crossed at the ankles instead of completely overlapping is an Amaravati influence. The head of the Dong Si Maha Pot image is true to the Mon style, with a rounded *ushnīsha*, the arched, joined eyebrows, the half-closed eyes, the flat nose, and the smiling mouth.

A type of iconography that is known only in the Mon art of Thailand and nowhere else in the Buddhist world represents the Buddha riding on a mythical animal (Plate 2). The meaning

2. Buddha Riding on a Mythical Animal. Stone; ht 38 cm. Mon art, Nakhon Pathom school, ninth to tenth centuries. National Museum, Bangkok. Photograph courtesy of the Stratton–Scott archives.

of such an image is unknown. One theory is that it is a derivation from the Hindu god Vishnu's riding on the giant bird, Garuda. By appearing on a similar vehicle, the Buddha may have become a symbol of the same universal royal power embodied in Vishnu. In another theory the Buddha is deemed to be descending from Tāvatimsa Heaven, where he had gone to teach his mother, although no text has been located that can justify such a vehicle. The texts, when referring to the descent from heaven, describe a set of three staircases, with the Buddha descending in the centre and the gods Indra and Brahma on either side. These Hindu gods are probably the attendants on this Mon relief. The figure on the Buddha's right is wearing a crown, typical of Indra. The one on the left wears his hair bound high on his head, the usual method for depicting Brahma. The Buddha lived in a milieu that shared a belief in the ancient gods of India. At the time that the Buddha lived, Indra, the king of the gods, and Brahma, the creator, were two of the most prominent. The Buddha neither denied nor affirmed the existence of gods. When he was asked whether there were gods, he invariably answered that that was an irrelevant question, that a searcher for the truth should be asking why did pain and suffering exist and how could these be eliminated.

The beasts in these Mon reliefs vary. This one has the horns of a bull, the remains of a garuda's beak, and the wings of a goose. The Buddha stands with his two hands in *vitarkamudrā*, the gesture traditionally interpreted by the Thai as signifying the descent from heaven. The robe is draped in the usual Mon manner, covering both shoulders and arranged symmetrically, falling in a pronounced U-curve in the front.

Mon art ceased in Central and North-east Thailand in the tenth century under the impact of Khmer influence. Further north, at a Mon centre called Haripunjaya (modern Lamphun), Buddha images continued to be produced into the thirteenth century. The style had clearly evolved from the Mon art of Central Thailand, but the faces were more square, a band framed the face along the hair-line, probably a Khmer influence, and the *ushnīsha* was conical and topped by a knob or a lotus bud. The head swelled above the temples but was flat on the top. The curls were small and spiky. The eyebrows were more horizontal than in the Central Thai style, but were still joined. The upper eyelids were straight. The nose was broad. The mouth resembled the Central Thai counterparts, but an incised line carved out a moustache. Haripunjaya also produced a number of crowned Buddha images which reflect styles imported from India during the Pala period (seventh to twelfth centuries) and from the Pagan art of Burma (eleventh to thirteenth centuries). These Haripunjaya images influenced some of the early Thai styles that we shall examine in the next chapter.

Khmer Styles

At times, certain areas of ancient Thailand were controlled politically by the Khmer people, whose centre was located at Angkor, south of the Dangrek Range which separates present-day Thailand from Kampuchea (Cambodia). Khmers of Hindu persuasion seem to have been present at Si Thep in the border-lands between Central and North-east Thailand by the late sixth century. In the eighth century, Khmers produced some out-standing Mahāyāna Buddhist art in the area just north of the Dangrek Range. Their presence is noted in that area again in the tenth century. By early in the eleventh century, Khmer power had extended over the whole of Central Thailand, with Lop Buri as the regional seat. This power continued until the thir-teenth century, when the Thai gradually displaced the Khmer. Khmer influence was greater in North-east Thailand, where much of the art may have been produced directly under Angkor control. Lop Buri in Central Thailand was further away, so its art tended to be a local variant of metropolitan models. In either case, the Khmer art of Thailand reflects the various art styles of the capital.

The ancient rulers of Kampuchea were generally Hindu, primarily supporters of Shiva. However, in the Khmer areas of North-east Thailand from the eighth to the thirteenth centuries, Mahāyāna Buddhism was the important faith. Early in the twelfth century, a Vajrayānist temple was erected at Phimai in Nakhon Ratchasima Province. In Central Thailand, even though Mahāyānist tendencies are discernible, the major faith continued to be Hīnayāna Buddhism.

A most important contribution made by the Khmer was the idea of decorating the Buddha with a crown and princely ornaments. Two major types were produced—one standing in regal majesty, the other seated under the protection of the naga. The earliest crowned Buddhas of Thailand were depicted on lintels at Prasat Phimai, Nakhon Ratchasima Province, Northeast Thailand. This temple can be dated by inscription to AD 1108, falling within the Early Angkor Wat style of Khmer art, a period which extended from about AD 1100 to 1150, according to the classification established by Piriya Krairiksh. Standing crowned Buddhas and also seated ones in *dhyānamudrā*, *bhumisparshamudrā*, and sheltered by the naga are all present at Phimai.

The standing crowned Buddha on the west lintel of Phimai is included here as Plate 3, a photograph taken by the Thai Fine Arts Department earlier in this century, before the face and crown were mutilated. This image reveals a kinship to Mon prototypes in its frontal stance, the robe covering both shoulders, and the hands, now broken, being held in identical positions, probably *vitarkamudrā*. However, the figure wears a diadem, a conical *ushnīsha* covered with a cap, and an ornate belt decorated with pendants. The latter supposedly supports the undergarment but appears to be placed over the outer robe.

1. Phra Buddha Jinarāja. Gilded bronze; ht *c.*300 cm. Thai–Sukhothai art, post-classic period, after AD 1425. Wat Mahathat, Phitsanulok. Photograph courtesy of the Stratton–Scott archives.

2. Standing Buddha, found at Korat, Nakhon Ratchasima Province. Bronze; ht 29.5 cm. Sri Lankan art, Anuradhapura period, eighth century. National Museum, Bangkok. Photograph courtesy of the Stratton–Scott archives.

3. Standing Buddha, found in Wiang Sa District, Surat Thani Province. Sandstone; ht 16.5 cm. Gupta art, Sarnath or Peninsular school, late fifth century. National Museum, Bangkok. Photograph courtesy of John Listopad.

4. Standing Buddha Bestowing a Blessing, Sarnath, India, given by the Government of India to HRH Prince Damrong Rajanubhab. Buff-coloured sandstone; ht 119 cm. Gupta art, late fifth century. National Museum, Bangkok. Photograph courtesy of the Stratton–Scott archives.

5. Standing Buddha. Bronze; ht 21.1 cm. Mon art, Central Thai style, eighth century. Nelson–Atkins Museum of Art, Kansas City, Missouri (Nelson Fund). (51–23).

6. Standing Buddha, from Wat Yai, Ban Ko, Nakhon Si Thammarat Province. Stone; ht 86 cm. Peninsular art, Mon style, eighth century. Wat Mahathat, Nakhon Si Thammarat. Photograph courtesy of the Stratton–Scott archives.

7. Buddha Protected by the Naga, from Dong Si Maha Pot, Prachinburi Province. Stone; ht 75 cm. Mon art, Dong Si Maha Pot school, seventh to eighth centuries. National Museum, Bangkok. Photograph courtesy of John Listopad.

8. Crowned Standing Buddha, from Wat Ratburana, Ayutthaya. Bronze; ht 41 cm. Khmer art, Angkor Wat style, late twelfth century. National Museum, Ayutthaya. Photograph courtesy of the Stratton–Scott archives.

9. Detail of Colour Plate 8; head. Photograph courtesy of the Stratton–Scott archives.

10. Buddha in Meditation, from Wat Phra Baromathat, Chaiya District. Stone; ht 104 cm. Peninsular art, Peninsular States period, sixth century. Chaiya National Museum, Chaiya. Photograph courtesy of John Listopad.

11. Standing Buddha, from Wat Chom Thong, Sichol District, Nakhon Si Thammarat Province. Bronze; ht 20.3 cm. Peninsular art, South Indian Later Amaravati influence, ninth century. National Museum, Nakhon Si Thammarat. Photograph courtesy of the Stratton–Scott archives.

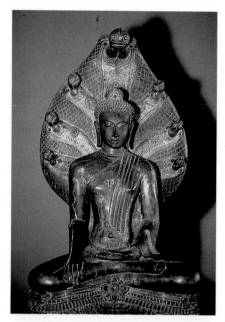

12. Buddha Protected by the Naga ('Buddha of Grahi'), from Wat Wiang, Chaiya District. Bronze; ht 160 cm. Peninsular art, Central Thai–Khmer style, dated AD 1183 or 1291. National Museum, Bangkok. Photograph courtesy of John Listopad.

13. Seated Buddha. Bronze; ht 60.3 cm. Thai–Lan Na art, lion type, fifteenth century. Nelson-Atkins Museum of Art, Kansas City, Missouri (Nelson Fund). (59–16).

14. Standing Buddha, from Wat Baromathat, Chai Nat Province. Gilt bronze; ht 117 cm. Thai–Lop Buri art, mid-thirteenth century. Chainatmuni National Museum, Chai Nat. Photograph courtesy of the Stratton–Scott archives.

15. Seated Crowned Buddha, from Lop Buri Province. Bronze; ht 21.2 cm. Thai–Lop Buri art, early thirteenth century. James H. W. Thompson Collection, Bangkok. Photograph courtesy of the James H. W. Thompson Foundation and the Stratton–Scott archives.

16. Three Crowned Buddhas under Arches, from Udayadhani Province. Bronze; ht 35 cm., w 28 cm. Thai–Lop Buri art, thirteenth to fourteenth centuries. National Museum, Bangkok. Photograph courtesy of the Stratton–Scott archives.

17. Seated Buddha, found in the crypt of Phra Prang at Wat Ratburana, Ayutthaya. Bronze with traces of gilt; ht 41 cm. Thai–Sankhaburi art, late thirteenth to fourteenth centuries. Chao Sam Phraya National Museum, Ayutthaya. Photograph courtesy of the Stratton–Scott archives.

18. Walking Buddha, found in the crypt of Phra Prang at Wat Ratburana, Ayutthaya. Bronze; ht 50 cm. Thai–Ayutthaya art, late fourteenth or early fifteenth century. Chao Sam Phraya National Museum, Ayutthaya. Photograph courtesy of the Stratton–Scott archives.

19. Standing Crowned Buddha. Bronze; ht 77 cm. Thai–Ayutthaya art, sixteenth century. Chantarakhasem National Museum, Ayutthaya. Photograph courtesy of the Stratton–Scott archives.

3. Western Lintel of Main Prang, Phimai, Nakhon Ratchasima Province, Thailand. Detail showing a standing crowned Buddha in a palace scene (before vandalism of the face and crown). Khmer art, early Angkor Wat style, AD 1108. Photograph courtesy of the Stratton–Scott archives, from a Thai Fine Arts Department original.

The undergarment also displays a central fold, visible through the outer robe. These decorative elements have evolved from Khmer Hindu imagery of the eleventh century.

Crowned Buddhas appeared frequently in Indian art, especially during the Pala period beginning in the seventh century. As early as the fifth century, in the caves of western India, flying deities held a crown over the head of a sculpted Buddha. Before crowned Buddhas were created, removable ornaments were occasionally added to images that were wearing only monastic robes. Such a practice was witnessed by the Chinese pilgrim Xuanzang during his travels in India in the early seventh century. The Mahāyānists and Vajrayānists, who worshipped side by side with the Hīnayānists in the same monasteries, may for special ceremonies have added ornaments to an existing image used by the earlier faith. Or perhaps the ornaments were applied merely to show respect to the image. Or again, crowning and decorating an image may have related to the Mahāyānist idea of the Buddha as a *chakravartin*, a universal emperor, reigning in glory over the universe. A crowned and decorated Buddha might also represent Vajradhara or Vajrasattva, emanations of the supreme Buddha of the Vajrayānists, the Adi-Buddha. The five great regional Buddhas of the Mahāyānists–the Tathāgatas–are also sometimes depicted in a decorated form. However, these are usually seated and perform specific hand gestures which help to identify them.

The meaning of the crowned Buddhas found in Thailand is not clear. Phimai was a centre of Vajrayāna Buddhism, so it is conceivable that the image there represented the Adi-Buddha, the Supreme Buddha. But more likely the crowned Buddhas both of Phimai and from other Khmer centres were inspired by purely Mahāyānist concepts. For example, Buddhas protected by the naga, some crowned and some uncrowned, are plentiful in Khmer art. Often such an image is the central figure of a trinity consisting of a Buddha, the bodhisattva Lokeshvara, a form of the greatest bodhisattva, Avalokiteshvara, and the female bodhisattva Prajnāpāramitā. In these trinities, the Buddha represents the abstract idea of buddhahood, the bodhisattva embodies the Mahāyānist concept of a compassionate being who helps all other beings achieve buddhahood, and Prajnā-pāramitā signifies the wisdom that allows one to attain buddhahood. At other times, as in India, the crowned Buddha may suggest the universal power of the Buddha, comparing him to a universal emperor presiding over the universe, which is another Mahāyānist idea.

The standing crowned Buddha depicted in the Phimai relief (Plate 3) seems to be in the setting of a great emperor surrounded by his attendants. There is a palace to the right, not included in this photograph. This scene may therefore be a representation of the Buddha as a *chakravartin*–a universal emperor–a role which is attested in Khmer epigraphy. Hiram Woodward, Jr. has suggested that this crowned Buddha on the western lintel at Phimai may be expressing the martial powers of the central Buddha of the temple,[5] which was almost certainly a Buddha protected by a naga who represented the supreme Buddha. Such an interpretation is consistent with the known Vajrayāna associations of the Phimai temple.

Others have suggested that the Phimai lintel may illustrate the story of Jambupati, a legend that is popular in Burma, Thailand, and Laos. This legend relates how the Buddha converted a proud emperor named Jambupati by transforming himself into an even more glorious and more sumptuously clad emperor in order to get Jambupati's attention. He was then able to preach to him and convert him. The Burmese call their crowned Buddhas Jambupati images, although in the tale Jambupati is the one being converted. It is not the name of the Buddha himself. Versions of the Jambupati story can be traced back to the fourteenth century, two hundred years after the erection of the temple at Phimai. The standing Buddha on the western lintel of the Phimai sanctuary more likely represents the Mahāyānist notion of the Buddha as a universal emperor.

The favourite term used by the Thai for a crowned and decorated image is Phra Chao Song Khruang–'a lord wearing ornaments'. Most likely in Thailand, even though the crowned Buddha began at Phimai and its cult spread from there, it has no deeper meaning than as a way of honouring the Buddha. To this day, the Emerald Buddha, currently the national palladium, is clothed three times a year in costly garments suitable for each of Thailand's three seasons, in a ceremony participated in by the King of Thailand himself. Creating a beautifully bedecked image expresses the same sentiment.

Crowned Buddha images became very widespread in Khmer art in the second half of the twelfth century, a period when the

---

[5] 'Studies in the Art of Central Siam, 950–1350 A.D.', Ph.D. dissertation, Yale University, 1975, p. 67.

Angkor Wat style was being disseminated throughout the Angkor kingdom's western provinces, including the Lop Buri area of Central Thailand. An example that can be dated to the middle of the century is the Buddha sheltered by the naga found at Wat Na Phra Men, Ayutthaya, and now in the National Museum, Bangkok (Plate 4). This Buddha sits in *dhyānamudrā* atop three coils of the naga king, whose seven-headed hood is spread over him. The Khmer face is more square than its Mon counterparts. The eyebrows are horizontal, still joined over the nose. The nose is wide and the lips thick. The Buddha wears a flaring diadem executed in the typical Khmer style, featuring a central band incised with a lozenge-shaped floral motif flanked by rows of rondels, and topped by a lotus-bud motif. The forehead is lined with a plain filet under a row of lotus petals. This filet dips over each temple. The large medallion at the centre front of the principal band of the diadem is a characteristic of provincial work. The *ushnīsha* is covered with a high conical cap decorated with rows of lotus petals between rondels. The Buddha also wears typically Khmer teardrop-shaped pendant ear-rings.

The early Khmer seated Buddha was usually depicted with a bare torso, another borrowing from the iconography of the Hindu images in the Angkor kingdom. On this example we can barely discern inscribed lines that indicate a robe covering the left shoulder only, and the third garment folded and placed across the shoulder. However, no sign of a robe is indicated in the space between the arms and the chest, nor on the wrists, so these inscribed lines may have been a later addition. The curving line of the undergarment is visible at the waist.

The style of the naga hood, swelling to its widest at the level of the Buddha's ears, and the six subsidiary heads turned toward the central one, are typical of the mid-twelfth century. So too is the way the knees of the Buddha extend beyond the coils of the naga, and the decreasing size of the three coils. The

4. Crowned Buddha Protected by the Naga, Wat Na Phra Men,
Ayutthaya. Granite; ht 184 cm. Khmer art, Angkor Wat style,
mid-twelfth century. National Museum, Bangkok. Photograph
courtesy of the Stratton–Scott archives.

Buddha still sits in *virāsana*, as in Mon art, but now the legs are laid straight across, right over left, rather than crossing at the ankles (compare with Colour Plate 7).

A standing crowned Buddha in the Angkor Wat style (late twelfth century) can be seen in Colour Plates 8 and 9. This bronze image is now in the National Museum, Ayutthaya. Like its Mon antecedents, this Buddha stands with rigid frontality, wearing a robe that covers both shoulders, thus maintaining the perfect symmetry so loved by the Mons. This is demonstrated both in the way that the corners of the robe are expressed, and also in the practice of having the two hands perform the same gesture—now the *abhayamudrā*—more typical than the *vitarkamudrā* in the latter part of the twelfth century. This Buddha has the square face, horizontal joined eyebrows, slender eyes, wide nose, and smiling mouth typical of Khmer pieces. His crown consists of a flaring diadem featuring the usual Khmer progression of a filet next to the forehead, topped by a row of rondels, a central band of diamonds and triangles, another row of rondels, and a top band of lotus petals which now has become saw-toothed. The diadem dips over the temples. The central medallion of the previous image has now become three, with the addition of two more over the ears. The conical *ushnī-sha* is covered with a cap, again decorated with lotus blossoms. The Buddha wears pendant ear-rings, and has added two wide necklaces with a quatrefoil medallion at the centre, plus a belt with a similar medallion and pendants. The centre fold of the undergarment is decorated with rondels and horizontal lines. Armlets appear on the upper arms.

A curious feature of this standing crowned Buddha—a feature typical of many of these images—is the fact that the ornaments appear to have been placed over the robe. Hitherto the undergarment, including the belt which holds it in place, has presumably been visible through the sheerness of the outer robe. Now the decoration of the vertical central fold seems to belong to the outer robe and the undergarment separately. Note the break at the level of the hem of the outer robe. The necklace and the armlets have clearly been placed over the monastic robe. This may be a consequence of the earlier practice of decorating an image in monastic garb with removable ornaments.

Piriya has labelled the decade from AD 1191 to 1200 as the late Angkor Wat and early Bayon transitional period. The period of dissemination of the Bayon style throughout the provinces followed in AD 1201–1219. During the Bayon period, there was a tendency to revert to the production of uncrowned images of the Buddha. A sandstone image from Prasat Phimai, now in the Bangkok National Museum, may serve as an example of the official style of the early Bayon period, AD 1191–1200 (Plate 5). This image, which was originally sheltered by the naga but now has the hood missing, reflects the typical Bayon-period sensibilities, including an expressive face with lowered eyelids and a smiling mouth, and hair curls arranged symmetrically, rising into a barely conical *ushnīsha*. The squarish face and the band bordering the forehead are typical Khmer features. The image is dressed in an outer robe that covers the left shoulder only. The fabric is visible between the left arm and the chest and over the wrist. The edge of the robe is indicated at the neckline as if it covered both shoulders, but it is obviously absent over the right arm. The undergarment is visible at the waist but there are no traces of it at the ankles. The knees of the Buddha still extend beyond the uppermost coil of the naga, but now the three coils are approximately the same size.

The Buddhas seated on a naga of the Bayon period, whether crowned or uncrowned, no longer illustrate the narrative of the Buddha's protection by the serpent king Muchalinda. Rather, such a Buddha was usually the central figure of the Mahāyānist triads discussed above, embodying the abstract idea of buddhahood.

45

5. Buddha Protected by the Naga (hood missing), Prasat Phimai, Nakhon Ratchasima Province. Green sandstone; ht 113 cm. Khmer art, Bayon style, late twelfth century. National Museum, Bangkok. Photograph courtesy of the Stratton–Scott archives.

Peninsular Styles

Piriya has subdivided the art of the Thai Peninsula preceding the thirteenth-century arrival of Thai art into four phases: the Indianized period (third to fifth centuries AD); the Mon and Peninsular States period (fifth to eighth centuries); the Indo-Javanese period (eighth to eleventh centuries), and the Khmer period (eleventh to thirteenth centuries). Both Brahmanical and Buddhist art were produced. We shall here be focusing on the Buddha images.

The location of the Peninsula straddling the trade routes between the Indian Ocean and the Gulf of Siam resulted in a great deal of Indian influence upon the arts and culture of the area. During the Indianized period, some sculptures and bronzes appear to have been imported directly from India into southern Thailand. We have already examined a Buddha from Wiang Sa District, Surat Thani Province (Colour Plate 3), which was either an import from Gupta India or modelled very closely after a Gupta example, datable to the late fifth century. The images found on the Peninsula that are datable from the third to the fifth centuries reflect the Gupta style of North India, the Andhra style of the south, or the style of Sri Lanka. Most were probably imported directly from one of those areas.

During the Mon and Peninsular States period, the Peninsula was divided into a number of small states, with Mon-speaking states in the northernmost area at the head of the Gulf of Siam. Commerce was beginning to be conducted by native traders as well as by Indians, and indigenous art was being produced. The sculpture was still closely linked with Indian models at this stage, although the results sometimes represent a hybrid of influences from different parts of India.

As a representation of the Mon art of the Peninsula, we have already examined a standing Buddha discovered at Wat Yai, Ban Ko, Nakhon Si Thammarat, datable to the eighth century (Colour Plate 6).

Chaiya was the most important of the Peninsular States during this period. Among its earliest productions is a stone Buddha from Wat Phra Baromathat, now in the Chaiya National Museum (Colour Plate 10). This image dates to about the sixth century AD, and is one of the earliest Buddhas produced in Thailand. The Buddha is seated in *virāsana* on a lotus. He performs the gesture of meditation (*dhyānamudrā*). His gentle smile and lowered eyes promote a feeling of deep introspection and tranquillity. He follows models from the Amaravati area of India or from Sri Lanka in the draping of his robe, with one shoulder only covered, and also in his hair treatment, with large curls and a barely discernible *ushnīsha*. The massive shoulders, the stance and solidity, and the way the legs are folded are reminiscent of Sri Lankan models.

The Indo-Javanese period, from the eighth to the eleventh centuries, was a time of close contact between the Peninsula and Java. Both areas were ruled by branches of the same Shailendra dynasty, the Peninsula being included in a maritime kingdom called Shrivijaya, which also encompassed the Indonesian island of Sumatra. During the Indo-Javanese period there was also a great deal of Mahāyāna and Vajrayāna religious and artistic influence directly from the Buddhist centre at Nalanda in North-east India, which was under the sway of the Pala dynasty. Many of the bronze seated Buddhas and bodhisattvas found on the Peninsula reflect strong Pala characteristics, which emanated either directly from Nalanda or indirectly from Java.

On the other hand, there is a type of standing Buddha from this period which suggests that influences were still entering the Peninsula from the Andhra area of South India, where a style known as Later Amaravati was being produced in the seventh to eighth centuries. We earlier examined a bronze Buddha found at Korat (Colour Plate 2), which combined this style with that of Sri Lanka. An image from Wat Chom Thong, Sichol District, Nakhon Si Thammarat Province (Colour Plate 11) is similar to the Korat Buddha and also to one from Buddhapad in the Andhra region in the Later Amaravati style (Plate 6). All three images have their robes draped in the Mathuran mode, with the entire end of the robe thrown back over the shoulder, falling to the level of the lower hem in the back. The robe of the Korat image reveals heavy striations, whereas the textile of the garment of the Buddhapad Buddha is smooth, with the folds not depicted. However, some Buddhas found at Buddhapad do display light striations suggesting folds, similar to those on the robe of the Wat Chom Thong image (Colour Plate 11).

The modelling of the form of the body beneath the sheer robe of the Buddhapad image is an influence from the Gupta school of Sarnath, possibly percolating to the eastern Andhra region through the art of the western caves (Plate 1). The image from Wat Chom Thong has been modelled in the same fashion as the Buddhapad image, except that the figure is more elongated and the stance more rigid. The hair arrangement with a low *ushnīsha* and the facial expression and modelling of the ears are similar on these two images.

The left hand of the Wat Chom Thong image holds the original end of the robe. The left hand of the Buddhapad image is now missing, but it too was probably holding the end of the robe. But the right hand gestures of these two images differ. That of the Buddhapad image is lowered in the gesture of offering charity, whereas the Wat Si Chom image has a bended elbow, suggesting either *vitarkamudrā* or *abhayamudrā*. The use of *vitarkamudrā* with the right hand and the left holding the robe are commonly encountered in both the Later Amaravati school of South India and in the contemporary school of Sri Lanka. The Wat Si Chom image was probably locally produced on the Peninsula, combining various Gupta, Post-Gupta, Later Amaravati, and Sri Lanka influences. This image should be dated to about the ninth century.

The major art period on the Peninsula during the eleventh to thirteenth centuries was Khmer. The Khmers did not extend political control over much of the Peninsula, but cultural

6. Standing Buddha, Buddhapad, Andhra Pradesh, India. Bronze; ht 38 cm. Later Amaravati style, seventh to eighth centuries. British Museum (OA 1905.12–18.1). Photograph courtesy of the Trustees of the British Museum.

influences did penetrate the region. The various Khmer sub-styles already examined in Central Thailand were present on the Peninsula as well.

An image which reflects a link with the final expression of Khmer art in Central Thailand is the well-known Buddha of Grahi (Colour Plate 12), discovered at Wat Wiang in Chaiya District on the Peninsula. This image has on its base an inscription in the Old Khmer language in Old Sumatran script, which states that the image was commissioned by the governor of Grahi on behalf of the king of Malayu, a kingdom in Sumatra that was the successor to Shrivijaya. Grahi has been variously hypothesized as a state in the Tha Chin Valley of Central Thailand, or as an alternate name for Chaiya. The date on the inscription has been interpreted both as AD 1183 and AD 1291, with more recent scholarship leaning toward the latter. We need more evidence before we can definitively date this Buddha image.

The Buddha of Grahi sits in *bhumisparshamudrā* sheltered by the naga. In Khmer art, the Buddha protected by the naga usually performed the meditation gesture, with the two hands resting on the lap, the gesture appropriate to the legend of the naga-king Muchalinda's protection of the Great Sage as he sat meditating on the shores of Lake Muchalinda during the third week after his enlightenment. The Khmers retained this gesture when they transformed the Buddha seated on the naga into a symbol of universal buddhahood in the triad groups. Associating the *bhumisparshamudrā* with a Buddha on the naga cannot be justified by the texts. The practice began in late Mon and late Khmer art in the Tha Chin Valley in Central Thailand. The images produced there may have served as prototypes for the Grahi Buddha. Piriya has suggested that the use of the touching-the-earth gesture in the case of the Buddha of Grahi and other thirteenth-century images of Central Thailand may have been a device of the Hīnayāna Buddhists of that area to distinguish their Buddhas being protected by Muchalinda from the central

Buddhas of the Khmer triads, which had usurped the *dhyāna-mudrā* iconography. The *bhumisparshamudrā* was becoming more popular generally for seated images in Thailand as a result of influences from North-east India during the Pala period (seventh to eleventh centuries; see Plate 11). The gesture was transferred to the Buddhas on the naga as well, even though in the Muchalinda story the Buddha was in deep meditation.

The Buddha of Grahi is dressed in the 'reversing inflection' (Figure 4), with the original end of the robe brought across the left shoulder to the front and over the left arm. The pleated portion near the centre looks as if it were the edge of that robe-end. However, a glimpse at the back of the image suggests it is the third garment (*sanghātī*) laid across the shoulder on top of the robe. This method of draping the robe may have been an influence from the Thai imagery concurrently being produced at Sukhothai in northern Thailand, which we shall explore in the next chapter.

In addition to its iconography, this image also relates stylistically to the late Mon- and Khmer-style sculptures of the twelfth and thirteenth centuries produced in the Tha Chin Valley of Central Thailand. The position of the legs, with the knees advanced and the ankles retracted, the tall erect torso, the squareness of the face, the bonnet shape of the hair arrangement, the snouted faces of the naga, the form of the naga coils, the lotus seat and the mat beneath it—above the uppermost coil of the naga—and the language of the inscription are all features of the Khmer art of Central Thailand. A Peninsular feature is the plain hemispherical *ushnīsha* with a bodhi leaf-shaped ornament at the front of it.

As we have seen, the Thai Peninsula has been a crossroads of many influences. By the fourteenth century, after the Thai kingdom founded at Ayutthaya had spread its hegemony over the entire nation, the art of the Peninsula merged into the national style. In the next chapter, we shall examine that style after first looking at earlier styles of art produced by the Thai.

3
The Thai Images

THE Thai people emerged as a political power in the mid-
thirteenth century. Their ancestral home had been located in
South-east China, from whence they slowly migrated over
several centuries into present-day Yunnan in South-west
China and also into the upper portions of Burma, Thailand,
and Laos. Their southward movement is clothed in mystery.
Recent studies of burial remains in Central Thailand suggest
that there has never been a decided change in the nature of the
people living in the area. It is possible that the indigenous
population was merely subjected to various overlords throughout its history–first the Mons, then the Khmer, and finally the
Thai. All of these groups and others have become amalga-
mated into the modern Thai citizen.

Sukhothai Style

The earliest of the new Thai kingdoms to produce an important school of art was Sukhothai, located in North Central Thailand. Two local kings in the mid-thirteenth century declared
their independence from their Khmer overlords, and one of
them was crowned by the other as the ruler of Sukhothai. The
third king of this dynasty, a son of the founder, was Ram
Kamheng (c.1279–98), who expanded the boundaries of the
kingdom to encompass most of present-day Thailand. He was
followed by Lo Thai (1298–1346/7), who lost some of the
territory, and Li Thai (1347–68/74). The classical period of
Sukhothai sculpture occurred during the reign of Li Thai, in
the mid-fourteenth century. This king entered into an alliance
with a newer Thai state to the south, Ayutthaya. Almost a century later, in 1438, Sukhothai was fully incorporated into

Ayutthaya and lost its own identity. The history of Sukhothai, therefore, was a short one of less than two centuries. However, the art styles first introduced during the Sukhothai period exercised tremendous influence on all the subsequent art styles in Thailand.

Important developments in Buddhism occurred during the Sukhothai period. The earlier people of Central Thailand, the Mons, had primarily been Hīnayāna Buddhists. The Thais had adopted this faith by the time they had gained political hegemony in Thailand, probably as a result of exposure to the Mons either at Dvaravati or Haripunjaya. Theravāda influence from Sri Lanka was brought to Sukhothai by King Ram Kamheng from the Peninsular state of Nakhon Si Thammarat, which he had incorporated into the Sukhothai kingdom. He invited a renowned monk from Nakhon Si Thammarat to become the Patriarch at Sukhothai. Under the next king, Lo Thai, additional Sri Lankan influence entered the monasteries of Sukhothai via contact with monks from Sri Lanka who were residing in the Mon kingdom of Ramannadesa in Lower Burma, and also through direct contacts between Sukhothai and the island nation.

The major contribution of the art of Sukhothai to the evolution of the Buddha image was the development of a fully in-the-round walking Buddha (Plate 7). Walking was one of the four positions deemed to be appropriate for a Buddha image, the others being standing, sitting, or reclining. The walking image had hitherto been rare. Only a few examples are known in India, always in relief. One can be seen at the right in the illustration of the façade of Cave 19 at Ajanta (Plate 1). Likewise, very few have been located in Sri Lanka and Burma. In Sukhothai, the walking Buddha became a common decorative element on the external walls of architectural monuments, included within a series of stucco reliefs, one on each face of the monument, depicting the Buddha in each of the four postures.

7. Walking Buddha, three-quarters view. Bronze; ht 220 cm. Thai–Sukhothai art, classic period, second half of the fourteenth century. Wat Benjama-bopit, Bangkok. Photograph courtesy of the Stratton–Scott archives.

An example of a stucco walking Buddha from Wat Mahathat, Chalieng, in the pre-classic, late thirteenth-century style, is depicted in Plate 8. During the reign of Li Thai and continuing throughout the second half of the fourteenth century, the Thai artisans created a fully in-the-round walking Buddha using the medium of bronze, a material which enabled them to translate the experience they had acquired in the modelling of stucco to the modelling of clay and its transformation into enduring metal.

The meaning of a walking figure is not always clear. In some bas-reliefs, the iconography is that of the descent of the Buddha from the Tāvatimsa Heaven, where he had visited his mother in order to teach her his doctrine. According to Pāli literature, he descended from heaven on a central jewelled ladder, flanked by the gods Indra and Brahma. This scene is portrayed on a well-known relief from Wat Trapang Tong Lang, Sukhothai.

Sri Lankan authors believe the walking figure represents a Buddha stamping his footprint into the ground, an influence of the Buddha's Footprint on Adam's Peak in Sri Lanka, which had become an important pilgrimage site by the time of the Polonnaruva period (1070-1235). The Sukhothai kings had created replicas of that footprint. A fifteenth-century example of a walking Buddha from the Lan Na kingdom in North Thailand, now in the Bangkok National Museum, clearly portrays Shākyamuni Buddha in the act of stamping his footprint on top of the footprints of the three Buddhas who had preceded him.

Griswold has suggested that the walking Buddhas of Sukhothai may have been the special talismans of the forest-dwelling sect of monks,[1] a group required to live at least a kilometre from the nearest town, necessitating a lengthy daily walk in

---

[1] *Towards a History of Sukhodaya Art*, Bangkok, Fine Arts Department, 1967, p. 24.

8. Walking Buddha, Wat Mahathat, Chalieng. Stucco relief. Thai–Sukhothai art, pre-classic style, late thirteenth century (?). Photograph courtesy of the Stratton–Scott archives.

order to collect food from the lay disciples. The forest-dwellers were especially favoured by King Ram Kamheng. It was this sect that he established by bringing an important forest-dwelling monk to Sukhothai from Nakhon Si Thammarat. Ultimately the influence had come from Sri Lanka. The walking Buddha seems appropriate as a symbol for these monks who lived in isolated monasteries. The static standing Buddhas, on the other hand, suggest the more limited activity of the town-dwelling monks who resided in the heart of the capital city. Griswold believed that Buddha images, including the method of draping the robes, reflect the doctrinal preferences of the monastic sects which created them.

The bronze walking Buddha now at Wat Benjamabopit, Bangkok (Plate 7), is the most famous example of this iconographical type. The weight of the figure rests on the left foot; the left leg forms a concave curve as it rises smoothly to the swollen hips. The heel of the right foot is lifted, and the heels of both feet project. The body has unusually wide shoulders and smoothly tapering arms that reach to the knee. The Buddha performs the gesture of teaching with his left hand while his right hangs at the side. This figure is asexual, with conspicuous nipples, full hips, and smooth limbs. A swollen bulge around the abdomen suggests the development of the muscles through yogic breath control. The hair is executed in small sharp curls, which dip slightly at the centre of the forehead and rise upward into a hemispherical *ushnīsha*, topped by a flame finial, a hallmark of the style (Plate 9). The eyebrows in the oval face are executed by a smooth ridge formed into two rounded arches, rising from the bridge of the nose. The eyelids are partially lowered in a gentle lotiform curve, extending upwards toward the temples. The nose is sharply pointed. The lips, demarcated by an incised line, with upward-turning corners, are gently smiling. The three lines on the neck are clearly visible. The ears are long and slightly pointed at the top.

9. Detail of Plate 7; head, profile. Photograph courtesy of the Stratton–Scott archives.

The Buddha is dressed in the open reversed mode, with the right shoulder bare, and the original end brought over to the front, its pleated edge ending in a fish-tail form at the level of the navel. Superimposed over this pleat is the tightly folded third garment (*sanghāti*). The front and back edges which fall from the left wrist meet together in a double ridge which descends in waves to the lower hem, where the corners bend forward in a little hook. A similar hook is visible at the Buddha's lower right. These hooks are hallmarks of the Sukhothai style. The way the robe spreads away from the body at the left and toward the back at the right helps to suggest the walking posture. The undergarment is not indicated at the waist, but is visible below the robe just above the ankles.

Many art historians have pondered upon the origins of the style of the walking Buddhas of Sukhothai. Some influences are detectable. From the Mon is derived the smoothness of the robe over the body, an idea which originated in the Gupta and Post-Gupta images of India. The method of draping the robe in the reverse mode, exposing one shoulder, was also known in Mon art, although the more usual Mon method was the covering of both shoulders, which was also the typical method for standing Sukhothai images. However, the lyrical, fluid style of the Sukhothai image is a decided contrast to that of Dvaravati (compare Plate 7 with the Cover Plate).

Very little Khmer influence can be detected (compare Plates 7 and 9 with Plate 5 and Colour Plate 8). The Sukhothai and the Khmer Buddhas contrast in almost every detail. The hair of a Khmer image is rendered in flat curls that rise to a conical rather than a hemispherical *ushnīsha*, and there is no flame. The hair-line of the Khmer image is outlined by a narrow band across the forehead. A shallow double arch, meeting at the bridge of the nose, represents the eyebrows. Both the nose and the mouth are broader. The ears are shorter. The face is more square.

The walking posture is unknown in Khmer art. If we compare a standing Khmer Buddha with the Sukhothai walking Buddha, we discover that the body of the Khmer Buddha is more stocky, and it lacks the smoothly flowing svelteness of the latter. There are differences in costume as well. The Sukhothai image has its robe draped over one shoulder instead of two, and it lacks the jewelled belt and decorated centre pleat of the Khmer image. Indeed, there is no articulation at all of the upper edge of the undergarment. The Sukhothai artists seem to have been attempting to break away completely from the Khmer style, perhaps to emphasize the state's political separation from its former overlords.

Sinhalese influence is likewise hard to find in the style of the Sukhothai walking Buddhas. The art of Sri Lanka stressed monumentality, with images most frequently rendered in stone, a more ponderous medium. There was Sinhalese influence in the flame finial which became a hallmark of the Sukhothai style. The flame, called a *ketumālā* or a *rashmi*, signifies the spiritual power and fiery energy of the Buddha, and is equivalent to a halo. A flame finial shaped like a lotus bud appeared on the Pala images of North-east India and in turn influenced the art of North Thailand (see Colour Plate 13). In South India, the flame can be seen on the eleventh- to thirteenth-century images produced at Nagapattinam. Such a finial was known in Sri Lanka as early as the eighth century and became very popular during the Polonnaruva (1070–1235) and Gampola (1341–1415) periods, the latter being the dynasty that was contemporary with the classic period of Sukhothai art and which exercised considerable influence over the architectural decoration of Sukhothai. The only previous image that we have encountered in this survey which has a flame finial is the small bronze from Korat (Colour Plate 2), which was an import from Sri Lanka. This characteristic possibly reached Sukhothai from Sri Lanka along with the new ideas in the Buddhist religion itself.

All Buddha images are a result of a conscious attempt to imitate a previous image in order to create a true likeness of the Buddha. The production of images of the Buddha has been traced back to a small steatite plaque found at Sankashya in Uttar Pradesh, India. This image, which is now lost, is stylistically datable to the Mauryan period, the third century BC and two centuries after the *parinirvāna* of the Buddha. There may have been earlier images, but none have survived. However, literary traditions, based upon apocryphal legends, extend the production of images back to the lifetime of the Buddha himself. Examples are a sandalwood image created by King Udayana of Kaushambi, another created by King Prasenajit at Shravasti, and images created by a fervent Buddhist householder, Anathapindaka. All of these were supposedly carved when the Buddha was absent for some reason and his lay followers wanted to be able to see him. These stories, whether spurious or not, illustrate that it was the lay people who were responsible for the production and setting up of Buddha images, rather than the monks who had been instructed to focus on the Buddha's teachings.

In spite of the tradition of copying existing images, the Sukhothai Buddha was primarily an innovation of the Thai artisans, rather than a derivation of preceding examples. Where did the ideas for this style originate? An artist traditionally studied existing models and then meditated deeply to create in his mind the image which he would then reproduce. It is believed that the Sukhothai artists combined the visual stimuli of known images with a fresh look at the descriptions of a Great Person in Pāli literature, perhaps as a result of the new contacts with Sri Lankan Buddhism, the source of the Pāli texts. The artist deliberately incorporated the prescribed features into his image. Thus the Buddha has 'projecting heels', 'his legs are like an antelope's', he can reach his knee with his hand, his skin is 'delicately smooth', his body is like that of a lion, and his bust is rounded. Secondary characteristics were incorporated as well: the sharp nose, the eyes shaped like the petals of a lotus, arms like the trunk of an elephant, fingers 'fine and tapering', feet 'smooth and regular', a deep navel, and no indication of muscles, veins, or bones. The use of bronze rather than stone also contributed to the Thai style. The artists model-led the form rather than chipped it out of stone, thus achieving greater fluidity and smoothness. The net result is one of the most beautiful depictions of the Buddha encountered any-where in Buddhist Asia.

A typical seated Buddha of classical Sukhothai art, now lo-cated at the National Museum, Bangkok, is depicted in Plate 10. The style of the face, the hair, the body, and the manner of draping the robe, including the fish-tail flap at the level of the navel, are all identical to that of the walking Buddha. The seat-ed Buddhas of Sukhothai are usually in *bhumisparshamudrā*, a gesture which the Sukhothai artisans probably borrowed from the Pala art of North-east India which influenced North Cen-tral Thailand by way of Burma and North Thailand (compare Plate 11 and Colour Plate 13). However, unlike the Pala-related images, the legs are not completely crossed in the *vajrāsana* pose. Rather, the right overlaps the left in *virāsana*, as encountered in Mon and Khmer art and ultimately derived from Sri Lanka. W. M. Sirisena has pointed out that the style of the folded legs, with a slight upward curve visible at the ankle of the upper leg, is similar to a twelfth-century image at Galvihara in Sri Lanka.[2] On most Khmer images (Plate 4) and those from Anuradhapura in Sri Lanka, the legs are perfectly horizontal. In Mon art the legs are withdrawn inward or else only the ankles are crossed (Colour Plate 7).

Most of the standing images of the classical period of Sukho-thai are of stucco and attached to architectural edifices. The icono-

[2] *Sri Lanka and South-East Asia*, Leiden, Brill, 1978, p. 146.

10. Seated Buddha. Bronze; ht 102 cm. Thai–Sukhothai art, classic period, second half of the fourteenth century. National Museum, Bangkok. Photograph courtesy of the Stratton–Scott archives.

graphy demands a far greater rigidity in the figure compared to that of the walking Buddha. The robe covers both shoulders, and the undergarment is rolled over the waist and held in place by a plain cloth belt. The central pleat forms another wide band descending down the front which, combined with the belt, results in a T-formation. This belt and pleat arrangement derived from late Mon and Khmer precedents, but at Sukhothai these elements are perfectly plain, not highly decorated as in Khmer art.

Reclining Buddhas are the most rare of the four postures for Buddha images in the Sukhothai style, as is true throughout the arts of the Buddhist world. These figures are interesting in the way they resemble a standing figure that has been laid on its side. The edge of the robe at the lower hem even extends into the air, defying the law of gravity! The style of the hair, face, and robe arrangement are all like that of the walking Buddha.

Lan Na (North Thailand) Styles

In 1292, a Thai chieftain named Mangrai, who had been ruling in Chiang Saen in the far north of Thailand, defeated the Mon kingdom of Haripunjaya and established a new kingdom called Lan Na. He set up his capital at Chiang Mai in 1296. Lan Na was an important kingdom until the mid-sixteenth century when it fell to the Burmese. It regained its independence sporadically, but was finally incorporated into Thailand in the nineteenth century. The golden age of the art of Lan Na occurred during the reign of King Tiloka (1441–87).

The most important Buddha images of Lan Na are seated ones, which were produced in two contrasting styles. One group has been labelled by Griswold as the 'lion-type' (Colour Plate 13), after the 'Lion of the Shakyas', the major image at the great Buddhist temple at Bodhgaya, India, the site of the Buddha's enlightenment. King Tiloka of Lan Na in the 1450s sent a delegation to Bodhgaya to bring back the plans of its famous temple. A replica, called the Seven Spires Monastery (Wat Chet Yot), was

erected in Chiang Mai. Since the Lan Na lion-type Buddha closely resembles images from North-east India (see Plate 11), it is highly probable that the delegation also brought back a copy of the
main image installed at Bodhgaya, and this copy became the
model for the hundreds of images produced in Lan Na. Alterna-
tively, these images could have arrived in North Thailand by way
of Pagan in Burma.

The lion-type Buddha is always seated with the legs fully crossed (*vajrāsana*) and with his right hand in the touching-the-earth
gesture (*bhumisparshamudrā*). His robe is draped over one shoulder only, and the third garment (*sanghātī*) is placed over the
shoulder, falling to above the nipple. On Pala images this shoulder
flap is more likely to be the pleated edge of the second garment
(*uttarāsanga*), the edge of which falls down the chest and across the
left arm, having been draped in the reverse mode. The hair of the
Lan Na lion-type Buddha is rendered in typical small curls, dip-
ping slightly at the centre of the forehead, and topped by a hemispherical *ushnīsha*, from which rises a *rashmi* in the form of a lotus
bud. The shoulders are wide, and the torso is plump with a roll
of flesh around the abdomen. The face is round. Comparatively
low arches, coming to a point at the bridge of the nose, shape the
brows. The eyes are half closed, with straight upper lids. The nose
is pointed. The lips are pursed. The demeanour is serious and
majestic, rather than genial and benign. The Buddha sits on a
lotus throne.

The second type of Lan Na image has been labelled by
Griswold as the 'mixed type'. These show Sukhothai influence
in the flame-like *ushnīsha*, a more oval face, the shoulder flap
reaching low past the navel, and the legs arranged in the *virāsana*
pose. This type, too, performs the touching-the-earth gesture.

Many art historians writing about the art of Thailand have
labelled the lion type as Early Chiang Saen, because they
thought these images had originated in the eleventh or twelfth
centuries before the founding of Lan Na. They believed that

11. Seated Buddha, Bihar, India. Schist; ht 63.5 cm. Pala art, tenth century. Nelson–Atkins Museum of Art, Kansas City, Missouri (Nelson Fund). (31–63).

these images preceded the mixed type, which they thus labelled as the Later Chiang Saen or Chiang Mai style. However, Griswold discovered that all the dated images of both types fall between 1470 and 1565, and overlap each other. Both were apparently being produced at the same time, the lion type influenced by the art of Pala India, perhaps through Pagan in Burma, and the mixed type influenced by Lan Na's southern neighbour, Sukhothai.

Lop Buri Style

At some time early in the thirteenth century, the principality of Lop Buri became independent of the Khmers and remained so until the founding of Ayutthaya in 1350, when Lop Buri was incorporated into that new kingdom. Piriya classifies as Lop Buri art those objects produced in Lop Buri during this brief period of independence. The art of Lop Buri was still strongly influenced by Khmer idioms but at the same time incorporated new ideas of the Thai people who were beginning to gain ascendancy.

An example of a standing Buddha in the Lop Buri style, datable to the mid-thirteenth century, is a gilt bronze now in the Chainatmuni National Museum in Chai Nat (Colour Plate 14). The robe is draped covering both shoulders. The undergarment is held in place by a wide belt. A centre panel, with the belt, forms a T or Y. The stocky proportions of this standing Buddha and the costume are inherited from Khmer art. Also Khmer are the details of the face, with its thick lips, cleft chin, wide nose, eyebrows that are largely horizontal, and lowered eyelids. The hair arrangement, consisting of tiny curls framed by a narrow band, and the conical *ushnīsha* covered with a cap decorated with receding levels of lotus petals, topped by a gem, are also Khmer idioms.

The right hand of this image, brought before the chest, is

in *abhayamudrā*, while the left hangs at the side with the palm outward. This combination of gestures is an influence from the Mon art of Haripunjaya. Buddhas performing these gestures were placed in the niches of the Haripunjaya monument at Wat Kukut in Lamphun when that monument was restored in AD 1218.

Crowned Buddhas were rare in the art of Sukhothai and of minor importance in Lan Na. But at Lop Buri, continuing the Khmer tradition, they were frequent and often in a new style. We have earlier seen the Khmer crowned Buddhas of Plate 4 and Colour Plates 8 and 9. The Khmer crown featured a wide flaring diadem and a cap over the conical *ushnīsha*. In the Lop Buri style of the early thirteenth century (Colour Plate 15), the bands of the diadem have been replaced by a series of long pointed leaves which alternate with a stalk motif. This type of crown also appeared in the late Mon art of Haripunjaya, and probably reached Lop Buri from that region. Ultimately the style had derived from Indian Pala antecedents, where the crowns regularly featured pointed leaves alternating with flower stalks. These elements on the Pala crowns had been both larger in size and fewer in number. At Haripunjaya and Lop Buri, the leaves and stalks became smaller, more numerous, and more elongated. The ear-rings, long and floral and flopping on to the shoulders, are also Pala. Pala, too, is the method of draping the robe, in the reverse inflection, with the final end brought forward across the left shoulder and down over the left arm. The third garment is placed across the shoulder, reaching almost to the navel. The conical cap covering the *ushnīsha*, the necklace, and the armlets of this image are Khmer features, as are the horizontal eyebrows. But the ovalness of the face and its other features, as well as the slenderness of the body, reflect Thai traditions. The elaborateness of the lotus seat and the arrangement of the robe in front of the legs are Pala idioms, but the posture, with overlapping rather than crossed legs, is typical of South-East Asia.

All in all, this crowned Buddha demonstrates a melding of ideas from many sources.

The art of Lop Buri also includes a number of crowned Buddhas seated in *bhumisparshamudrā* upon high decorated pedestals within elaborate little houses or tabernacles ('jewelled houses') called *ruan kaeo* in Thai or *ratnaprasāda* in Sanskrit. Sometimes these were single images and at other times a number of Buddhas were placed side by side (Colour Plate 16). These tabernacles represent a combination of Pala and Khmer influences. The Pala artisans had long placed their figures on elaborate pedestals, with flaming backpieces. But the tiered and recessed pedestal and the shape of the niche had appeared early in the Khmer tradition as well. Khmer artisans were expert at the art of bronze casting, and undoubtedly passed the technique to their provincial counterparts.

In the Hīnayāna tradition of South-East Asia, the depiction of multiple Buddhas suggests the Buddhas who appear successively in the universe, rather than the multitude of concurrent Buddhas more typical of Mahāyānist thinking. In North-east India during the Pala period, on the other hand, Mahāyāna and Vajrayāna Buddhism were the most typical forms of the religion. The two extra Buddhas at the top of the Pala stele (Plate 11) therefore probably connote the Mahāyānist beliefs.

Suphan Buri Style

Contemporary with the Lop Buri style in the second half of the thirteenth century, a different style of art was being produced at Suphan Buri, a bit further west in Central Thailand. This style, formerly classified as U Thong A, has been labelled by Piriya as the Suphan Buri style. The Buddha images from the Suphan Buri area combine Mon, Khmer, and Thai influences with late Mon elements from Haripunjaya. An excellent example is a bronze head now in the U Thong National Mu-

12. Head of a Buddha, Suphan Buri Province. Bronze; ht 24 cm. Thai–Suphan
Buri art, second half of the thirteenth century. U Thong National Museum. Photograph courtesy of the Stratton–Scott archives.

seum (Plate 12). The well-developed forehead, the almond-shaped eyes with straight eyelids barely lowered, the straight nose with nostrils slightly dilated, the serene mouth with the corners of the lips elevated, the strong chin, the modelling of the ear lobes, the tiny conical curls, and the bare, ogival *ushnī-sha* are all found in the late twelfth- to thirteenth-century Mon art of Haripunjaya in northern Thailand. The square forehead of the Suphan Buri head, the band lining the forehead, and the straightness of the eyebrows are Khmer characteristics. The naturalness of the facial features is a Thai contribution.

Sankhaburi Style

From the end of the thirteenth century until the third quarter of the fourteenth century, a style of art, formerly classified as U Thong B, was produced in the Sankhaburi area of Central Thailand. Sankhaburi images combine Khmer facial features and sobriety with a flame *ushnīsha* borrowed from Sukhothai. This flame always sits in a cup of lotus petals. This style is noted for its minuscule curls and for the elongation of the outline of the seated figure, the shoulders and knees having become narrowed in proportion to the height. An example from the Ayutthaya National Museum can be seen in Colour Plate 17.

Ayutthaya Styles

In 1350, a new Thai state emerged with its capital at Ayutthaya in Central Thailand. This state eventually extended its sway over all of present-day Thailand except the extreme north, and became the heir to the Sukhothai, Khmer, and various Central Thai traditions, amalgamating them all into a national style. Ayutthaya even defeated the Khmer state at Angkor and borrowed many Khmer cultural traditions directly from the source. Ayutthaya remained the dominant power in South-East Asia until 1767, when the kingdom was conquered by the Burmese and the capital destroyed.

The earliest Ayutthaya style, datable to the late fourteenth to mid-fifteenth centuries, was formerly called U Thong C. Images in this style incorporate a strong Sukhothai influence in the oval face and elongated body. An example can be seen in Plate 13. The silhouette of this Buddha is similar to that of the Sankhaburi bronze (Colour Plate 17), although slightly more attenuated. The face is decidedly more oval than square, thus moving away from Khmer influence. The features of the face, the flame atop the *ushnīsha*, and the placement of the folded shawl with its fish-tail end extending to the navel are all borrowings from Sukhothai. The band framing the hair and the unsmiling expression survive from Khmer traditions. The ring at the base of the flame is an innovation from the Sankhaburi art of Central Thailand. This image was one of several hundred discovered in the crypt of the main *prang* at Wat Ratburana in Ayutthaya, a structure dedicated in 1424.

Walking Buddhas were also created during the Early Ayutthaya period, in the late fourteenth to early fifteenth centuries. The example in Colour Plate 18, also found in the crypt at Wat Ratburana, is similar to the above seated Buddha in the elongation of its silhouette, the sobriety of its face, its ovalness, and the minuscule curls leading smoothly into a cylindrical *ushnīsha*, topped by a flame. The stance and gestures of this image are reversed from those of the Sukhothai walking Buddha previously examined (Plate 7). The weight is now on the right foot instead of the left, and the right hand is raised in the *vitarkamudrā*, with the left hanging down beside the body.

In the fully developed Ayutthaya style (Plate 14), the Buddha has become hieratic and aloof. The method of draping the robe, covering both shoulders, descends from Mon prototypes, as does the *mudrā*, with the two hands performing the same gesture in perfect symmetry. The presence of a belt and the promi-

13. Seated Buddha, crypt of the main *prang* of Wat Ratburana, Ayutthaya. Bronze; ht 55 cm. Thai–Early Ayutthaya art, late fourteenth to early fifteenth century. National Museum, Bangkok. Photograph courtesy of the Stratton–Scott archives.

14. Standing Buddha. Bronze; ht 25.5 cm. Thai–Ayutthaya art, late
fifteenth or early sixteenth century. National Museum, Bangkok.
Photograph courtesy of the Stratton–Scott archives.

nent central fold of the undergarment, arranged to form a T or Y, is a characteristic that runs throughout late Mon, Khmer, and Sukhothai art. The face is rounder than its Sukhothai or Central Thai prototypes, and the eyes, nose, and mouth are all wider. The band along the forehead is still present, but often disappears in the Ayutthaya style. It is absent on the walking Buddha of Colour Plate 18. The curls of this standing Buddha are minuscule. The ubiquitous flame tops the *ushnīsha*. This image dates to the late fifteenth or early sixteenth century.

Crowned Buddha images, which we have already encountered in Khmer and Lop Buri art, were also popular during the Ayutthaya period. The Buddhas of Suphan Buri, Sankhaburi, and Early Ayutthaya did not wear crowns. Crowns were rare on Sukhothai images as well. The few examples that are known are late and can more properly be labelled as Ayutthaya specimens. During the Ayutthaya period, such images could be rather restrained (*song khruang noi*) (Colour Plate 19) or extremely profuse in their decoration (*song khruang yai*) (Plate 15), with many stages in between (see the analysis of the types of the crowned Buddha images of Ayutthaya by Forest McGill[3]).

The earlier type, from the Chantharakhasem National Museum, Ayutthaya, is datable to the early sixteenth century (Colour Plate 19). The Buddha is dressed in monastic garb which covers both shoulders. He performs the gesture of *abhayamudrā* with his right hand, which in the Thai context came to mean calming his relatives. His left hand hangs at the side, palm inward. His *ushnīsha* is concealed under a high-tiered conical cover topped with a jewel. This is combined with a wide diadem-like band decorated with gems and filigree, with flanges over the ears. This band covers the temples at the front and descends to the lower edge of the hair-line at the back. This style of crown

---

[3] 'The Art and Architecture of the Reign of King Prasattong of Ayutthaya (1629–1656)', Ph.D. dissertation, University of Michigan, 1977, pp. 238–47.

15. Bejewelled Seated Buddha. Bronze; ht 98 cm. Thai–Ayutthaya art, late seventeenth century. National Museum, Bangkok. Photograph courtesy of the Stratton–Scott archives.

is derived from the crowns of Hindu images produced at Su-khothai, which were probably modelled after the crowns of the king. The side flanges on the crown were an innovation during the Ayutthaya period. The belt and central fold of this image are plain, and there is no jewellery other than the crown. The later crowned Buddhas of Ayutthaya added a wide neck-lace, a pectoral pendant or crossed bandoliers, a jewelled belt, armlets, anklets, and many other ornaments.

The culmination of the process resulted in an image such as the one depicted in Plate 15, on loan to the Bangkok National Museum from Wat Benjamabopit. This image was produced late in the seventeenth century. By this time the ornamenta-tion had become exaggerated. The figure is seated in *virāsana*, with his right hand in the touching-the-earth gesture and his left resting on his lap. He wears a high conical crown consisting of superimposed tiers of leaves, followed by a narrow section which widens again into more tiers of leaves, culminating in a tall, narrow, conical element. The diadem is decorated with a simi-lar row of leaves, flanked by rows of pearls. Sharp flanges ex-tend from the sides of this diadem. Additional flame-like pieces project from the crown just above and below the ears. This image also wears teardrop ear-rings, a wide necklace, two sets of armlets, bracelets, and extensive anklets. It is to be imagined that he is still wearing a monastic robe, draped over the left shoulder only. Note that the figure has not been hollowed out between the left arm and the body because that area is engulfed by the robe. Where the robe falls over the legs just below the knees, its hem is also elaborately decorated. A belt is visible at the waistline. The most conspicuous feature of the ornamenta-tion are the two bandoliers that fall from the shoulders and are drawn together on the chest by a diamond-shaped medallion, from under which two long flame-like devices protrude to-ward the sides. These two bandoliers are similarly fastened to-gether on the back of the image. The same leaf-like motif seen on the crown decorates the many ornaments.

These highly decorated crowned Buddha images of the later Ayutthaya period probably do not depict the supreme transcendent Buddha that may have been the motivation during the Khmer period. Rather, they now illustrate the story of King Jambupati, the great emperor converted by the Buddha referred to earlier. The Buddha magically clothed himself in sumptuous garments and costly ornaments to humble the pride of Jambupati so that the emperor would then open his ears to the doctrine and become converted.

Ratanakosin (Bangkok) Style

After the Burmese destroyed the capital city of Ayutthaya in 1767, the capital was moved southward, first to Thonburi on the right bank of the Chao Phya, and then in 1782 to Bangkok across the river. Bangkok was the seat established by King Rama I (1782–1809), the first ruler of the Chakri dynasty which still reigns in Thailand today. Rama I, busy with military conquest and the consolidation of his kingdom, concentrated on protecting existing images by gathering together some twelve hundred old images from all over the nation to install in the new monasteries of the capital. The few new images that were produced during his reign and that of Rama II (1809–24) adhered to the Ayutthaya style.

Among the images brought to the capital was the Emerald Buddha, a famous image which has undergone many peregrinations. It was discovered in a temple in Chiang Rai in North Thailand in the early fifteenth century, and was taken by the king of Lan Na first to Lampang and later to Chiang Mai. In the sixteenth century, a Laotian who had married into the Lan Na royal family took the image to Luang Prabang in Laos and later it moved on to Vientiane. King Rama I captured Vientiane and brought the Emerald Buddha back to Thailand, installing it first at Wat Arun in Thonburi and then in the Royal Chapel in Bangkok. This image, which is made of a greenish quartz rather than of emerald, and was probably created in Lan Na in the late fourteenth or early fifteenth century, is now the palladium of the Thai nation.

Another famous image that was brought to Bangkok during the reign of King Rama I was the Phra Phuttha Sihing, the Sinhalese Buddha, so-named because, according to legend, it originated in Sri Lanka, the home of the Sinhalese people. Its legend relates that it was magically created in Sri Lanka in the second century AD. In the thirteenth century, a Sukhothai king persuaded the king of Sri Lanka to send him the image. However, the ship carrying the image struck a reef and sank, and the image floated on a plank toward the shore of the southern Thai Peninsula. There it was rescued by the king of Nakhon Si Thammarat, and then taken north by the Sukhothai ruler. It became a part of the plunder of every military conqueror, and was moved frequently from one principality of North Thailand to another. Eventually it found a home in Chiang Mai, then later in Ayutthaya, then again in Chiang Mai. Finally, in 1795, it was brought to Bangkok and installed in the Wang Na, the Palace of the Front, the residence of Rama I's deputy king. This palace later became the nucleus of the National Museum. The Phra Phuttha Sihing resides today in the Buddhaisawan Chapel within the precincts of the National Museum. In addition to the image at Bangkok, there are images at Nakhon Si Thammarat and Chiang Mai that lay claim to being the Phra Phuttha Sihing. None of the three is in a Sri Lankan style. The image at Chiang Mai is in a fifteenth-century Lan Na style, that of Nakhon Si Thammarat is in a Thai style typical of that peninsular area, and the image in Bangkok is in the post-classic Sukhothai style of the fifteenth century. All of them are probably copies of a lost original Phra Phuttha Sihing, whatever its origin may have been. This image is still much loved by the Thai people. During the Songkran festival in the springtime, it is taken out on to the Pramane Ground in front of the National Museum, where every worshipper can sprinkle it with a few drops of water as a merit-making gesture.

Rama I installed a regnal image in the Royal Chapel, thereby continuing a custom inaugurated by earlier Thai rulers. Such an image is known as Phra Chai or Lord of Victory. The Buddha sits on an elaborate pedestal under a five-tiered umbrella, performing the touching-the-earth gesture, and holding a fan before his face in the manner of a monk in Thai society. The function of a Phra Chai image was to ensure victory for the ruler. It therefore accompanied the king on his military expeditions. Regnal images were created by each of the Chakri rulers except for Rama VIII, who died before his own consecration.

Rama I also set up Buddha images dedicated to various members of the royal family, continuing a custom that can be traced back to the period of Khmer occupation of Thailand in the twelfth to thirteenth centuries. His Chakri successors continued this practice. Many of these were standing Buddhas in royal attire, the decoration of which became ever more elaborate with a lavish use of gold, lacquer, enamel, and jewels.

During the reign of Rama III (1824–51), an attempt was made to expand the iconographical repertoire of the Buddha image. The King asked the patriarch to identify scenes in the life of the Buddha that were suitable for illustration. These were discussed in Chapter 1.

Beginning in the reign of King Rama IV (1851–68) and continuing into the twentieth century, some artists tried to create more realistic Buddha images. An outstanding example is the Phra Phuttha Khanthararat, or Gandharan Buddha, now in the Bangkok National Museum, which imitates the second- to third-century style of North-west India. The head of this image is in the ancient Gandharan style, which was strongly influenced by Hellenistic art. The hair is rendered naturalistically, gathered up into a rounded bun on top. The modelling of the body and the folds of the robe are likewise realistic, reflecting the aesthetics of the Gupta period more than the Gandhara. The combination of hand gestures performed by this image—reassurance with the right and charity with the left—is labelled by the Thai as invoking rain.

A further attempt at naturalism occurred in 1957 to celebrate the two thousand five-hundredth anniversary of the death of the Buddha. A stucco walking Buddha was created by Professor Silpa Bhirasri, an Italian artist who served in Thailand from 1933 until his death in 1962. Called 'the father of modern art in Thailand', this teacher was instrumental in establishing the School of Fine Arts, which became Silpakorn University, and introducing Western art forms to generations of Thai students.

Many paintings that feature images of the Buddha survive from the Ratanakosin period. Some of these are cloth banners that represent a Buddha flanked by two monks or two gods. The interior walls of the various religious halls in the temple compounds are filled with mural paintings, many depicting scenes from the Life of the Buddha. Illustrations of the Buddha performing various activities abound—preaching to gods, men and demons, walking, sitting with his disciples, lying down, or standing. Just inside the main entrance of nearly every ordination hall is a gigantic painted scene depicting the Buddha at the moment of his enlightenment, when he calls upon the earth goddess Thoranee to come forth to bear witness to the merit that he has accumulated throughout his many lives. The seated Buddha in *bhumisparshamudrā* is flanked by the armies of the demon Mara, who arrive in ferocious power at the right of the painting, and are washed away in the waters representing the great merit of the Buddha at the left, the flood having been wrung out of the hair of the goddess Thoranee, who appears at the bottom of the painting.

Any resident of Thailand, and even the most casual visitor, will soon feel that he is engulfed in images of the Buddha. They are everywhere—in temples and markets, in antique shops and curio stalls, in museums throughout the country, in homes, in business offices and private shrines, and on amulets around believers' necks. The images come in all sizes and postures and materials. They reflect at least fourteen centuries of active Buddhist history in the area of Thailand. Regardless of the medium, however simple or artful the style, or whatever the gesture or posture, they all reflect the great teacher who walked on earth over two thousand five hundred years ago and inspired the psychological and ethical teachings that became the Buddhist religion.

Select Bibliography

Boisselier, Jean, *The Heritage of Thai Sculpture*, New York, Weather-hill, 1975.

Bowie, Theodore, ed., *The Sculpture of Thailand*, New York, The Asia Society, 1972.

Piriya Krairiksh, *Art in Peninsular Thailand Prior to the Fourteenth Century A.D.*, Bangkok, Fine Arts Department, 1980.

_____, *Art Styles in Thailand*, Bangkok, Fine Arts Department, 1977.

_____, *Khmer Bronzes*, Lugano, Italy, Corner Bank, *c.*1984.

_____, *The Sacred Image: Sculpture from Thailand*, Cologne, Museum for East-Asian Art, 1979.

Stratton, Carol and Miriam McNair Scott, *The Art of Sukhothai*, Kuala Lumpur, Oxford University Press, 1981.

Subhadradis Diskul, M. C., *Art in Thailand: A Brief History*, 6th ed., Bangkok, Amarin Press, 1986.

Index

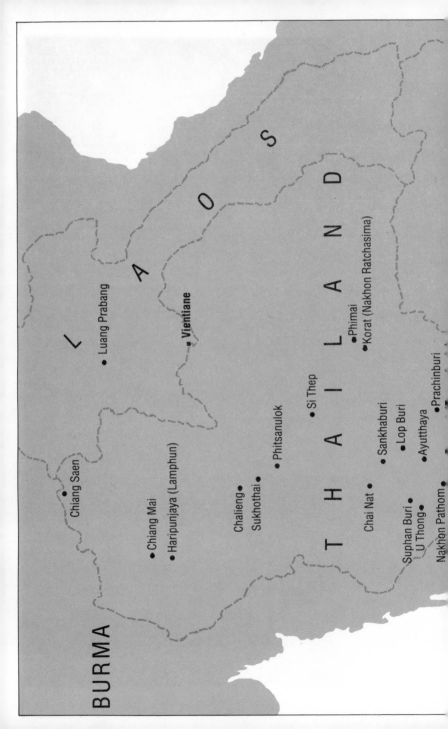